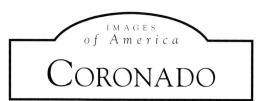

IMAGES
of America

CORONADO

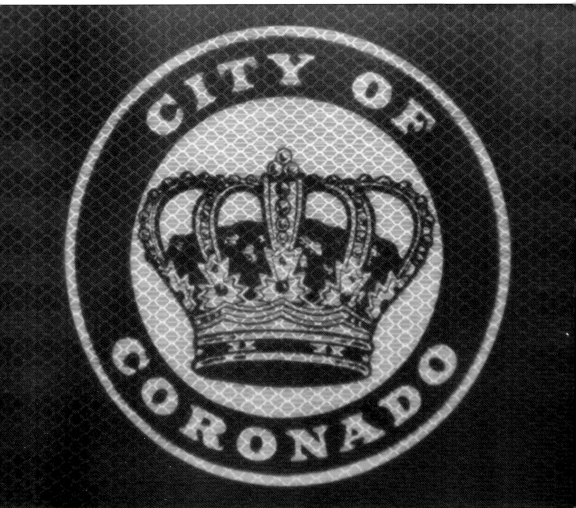

Coronado is the "Crown City." From the Coronado flag to the City of Coronado's incorporation logo, the crown has epitomized Coronado from its first days of occupation. The name *Coronado* was derived from the offshore islands Las Islas de los Coronados, which were named by an early explorer. (LHC.)

ON THE COVER: Taken around 1901, this photograph by F. E. Patterson shows families at Coronado Beach in Tent City, located just south of the Hotel del Coronado. Whether spending the summer or just the day, bathing suits could be rented for beachgoers. (SDHC.)

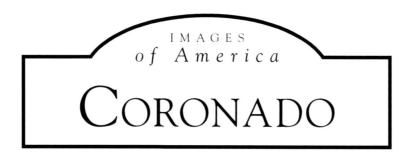

IMAGES
of America

CORONADO

Leslie Hubbard Crawford

ARCADIA
PUBLISHING

Published by Arcadia Publishing
Charleston, South Carolina

Printed in the United States of America

Library of Congress Control Number: 2010926122

For all general information, please contact Arcadia Publishing:
Telephone 843-853-2070
Fax 843-853-0044
E-mail sales@arcadiapublishing.com
For customer service and orders:
Toll-Free 1-888-313-2665

Visit us on the Internet at www.arcadiapublishing.com

Dedicated to all historians, past and present, personal and professional, who have lovingly collected, tended, and shared the history of this beloved little city, Coronado.

Contents

ACKNOWLEDGMENTS

When I started this project, my focus on finding images for the book led me to some interesting resources and introduced me to new friends.

The San Diego History Center has a staggering number of photographs and print materials. Chris Travers, director of photographs; Carol Myers, photograph archivist; and Jane Kenealy, document archivist, were invaluable with their help in locating resources. San Diego History Center photographs are credited as SDHC.

I am thankful to Susan Enowitz, director of the Coronado Historical Association, and Rachel Lieu, archivist at the Coronado Historical Association, for giving me the opportunity to look through their archives. I am also thankful to Marijean Crow, docent at the Coronado Historical Association, who gave me an insightful tour one beautiful morning in Coronado. Coronado Historical Association photographs are credited as CHA.

Coronado Public Library director Christian Esquevin and archivist Candice Hooper were extremely helpful and thoughtful in sharing their images and resources. Coronado Public Library's photographs are credited as CPL. The Public Affairs Office at Naval Base Coronado was helpful in sharing their classic images with me. Their images are credited US Navy.

Sue Gillingham, co-owner of the 1906 Lodge in Coronado, graciously shared with me the postcards, images, and other collectibles with which she had decorated the lodge's rooms. I enjoyed the many hours I sat in the parlor of the lodge scanning those images into my computer. Photographs provided by Sue Gillingham are credited as 1906 Lodge.

I also would like to sincerely thank everyone who shared their wisdom and photographs with me: Roger Clapp, Chip Maury, Barbara Reynolds Haines, Ky Winchester Roberts, Suzie Heap, Jean and Langdon Smith, John Elwell, Ben Siegfried, Marilyn Fulton, and John Munns. Though I could not use all the photographs they shared with me, I loved hearing their stories and I appreciate the time they gave. Photographs I did use are credited with the individuals' names, and images from my personal collection are credited as LHC.

A few books were instrumental in my research: *San Diego's Navy* by Bruce Linder; *Jackrabbits t.o Jets* by Elretta Sudsbury; and the definitive historical resource *Coronado: The Enchanted Island* by Katherine Eitzen Carlin and Ray Brandes. Old Coronado newspapers at the Coronado Public Library and copies of San Diego Union newspapers at San Diego History Center provided the bulk of information in this book.

My father, Don Hubbard, led me by example with his published books and stories from the writing "trenches." I inherited his tenacity, so I felt equipped when I started this project.

My family lived through the chaos of this project. Andrew typed, Mike did some research, and my husband, Don, did everything I forgot to do, or just plain did not want to do; in other words, he supported me unconditionally, so I could focus on the tasks at hand. A special thanks to the Field Hockey Girls who cheered me on during the final months of this project.

Lastly, I want to sincerely thank my editor, Debbie Seracini, who put a great deal of faith in me, a novice book author. Debbie gave me great guidance and encouragement, pushed me when I needed it, and pushed even harder as the conclusion neared. I thoroughly enjoyed authoring this book and thank her for allowing me the opportunity to do so.

As it usually happens with history projects, the compiling of this book opened more paths for research than it closed. I look forward to future investigations of Coronado in order to piece together the puzzle that is its history.

—L. H. C.
2010

INTRODUCTION

The first explorers sailing into San Diego Bay made more mention of the offshore islands than of the peninsula now known as Coronado. When Spanish explorer Juan Cabrillo sailed past the islands in 1542, he called them Las Islas Desiertas, "the Desert Islands." Decades later, Spanish explorer Sebastian Viscaino passed the islands on November 8, 1602, a holy day commemorating four Christian soldiers, known as "the Crowned Ones," who were martyred in the early fourth century. A priest on board the ship named the islands Las Islas de los Coronados in their honor.

The peninsula remained wild, home to jackrabbits and quail and covered with brush, yucca, and trees. Seals could be seen sunning themselves on the spit of land between the north and south islands. Freshwater wells provided potable drink for the natives who periodically lived at the south end of the peninsula, at the bottom of San Diego Bay, and probably passed through Coronado with the seasons.

California was admitted to the Union in 1850, after the Mexican-American War ended. Cattle were raised on the North Island area of the peninsula, and crops were farmed there also. Ownership of the peninsula changed hands a number of times from the 1850s to 1885, making the specific titles and rights of the land a bit cloudy.

In November 1885, Elisha Babcock, Hampton Story, and Jacob Gruendike, along with two other minority partners, purchased the peninsula for $110,000. Other investors lacked their winning combination of inspiration, entrepeneurial spirit, business connections, and financial backing that made their dream of developing the land a reality.

On April 7, 1886, the five partners filed articles of incorporation for the Coronado Beach Company, putting up $100,000 in capital. The peninsula was named Coronado after the Mexican islands offshore, Las Islas de los Coronados. Subsidiary companies under the umbrella of the Coronado Beach Company included the Coronado Beach Water Company, the Coronado Ferry Company, the Coronado Railroad Company, the Coronado Brick Company, and the San Diego-Coronado Transfer Company.

The Hotel del Coronado was constructed in 1887 with great anticipation and opened to much fanfare as the entire population of the Coronado peninsula grew rapidly. The hotel was instantly successful, but the cost of running it during an economic depression was financially draining. John Dietrich Spreckels and his brother Adolph B. Spreckels bought all the holdings of the Coronado Beach Company and took complete ownership of the hotel in 1892. John Spreckels's commitment to Coronado left a lasting legacy in the form of Spreckels Park, located directly across from the Coronado Public Library that he gifted to the City of Coronado in 1909.

Well-known for both the Hotel del Coronado and Tent City, a high-class camping area, Coronado became a playground for the wealthy, including celebrities and politicians. Families from around the country wintered at the hotel, many eventually moving permanently into homes on Coronado Beach. Tent City attracted crowds during the summer and provided fun for both residents of the peninsula and day visitors from San Diego and other outlying areas.

On December 9, 1890, Coronado was officially incorporated as a city. A board of trustees headed by a president governed Coronado until 1926 when a city council was formed and a mayor was appointed to office. In 1972, Coronado voters had their first opportunity to vote for mayor. Terms started at two years, but now last for four.

Two U.S. Navy bases influence Coronado, melding a cross-section of cultures and demographics that share an appreciation for Coronado's small-town feel, quality of life, and rich history. Naval Air Station North Island and Naval Amphibious Base are separate naval installations consolidated under the direction of the commanding officer, Naval Base Coronado.

Tourism continues to be the lifeblood of Coronado. Visitors notice Coronado's wide streets, beautiful gardens, and unique architecture. Its spectacular beach stretches for miles and is rated one of the top beaches in the United States. Civic duty is a popular trend in the area, and many service organizations and nonprofits lend a helping hand to the community. Long-standing traditions in Coronado include the annual flower show, summer concerts in the park, the Fourth of July parade and fireworks, the All-Class Reunion (which reunites generations of past and present Coronado residents), the Optimist Sports Fiesta (which boasts the longest continuous-running triathlon in the United States), and the annual Christmas parade during which a giant evergreen at the intersection of Orange Avenue and Tenth Street is lit by Santa Claus while the Coronado Community Band strikes up a rousing concert of Christmas carols.

Though residents of Coronado love their little city, historic documentation shows that through the years Coronado has had its share of issues that polarized the community: schools, politics, infrastructure, historic preservation, and military factors to name a few. The city's beloved ferries eventually gave way to a bridge that dramatically changed life on the peninsula. Residents feel strongly about preserving the quality of life for which Coronado is renowned but realize the need to balance tradition with tourism and development in order to keep the local economy strong.

Coronado's earliest years were established with the thought and ingenuity of men and women of vision who clearly saw Coronado as a unique opportunity. Babcock, Story, Gruendike, Horton, Marston, Sessions, and Spreckels are big names in the area's history. These smart, determined personalities converged in Coronado in a variety of ways, helping to create a resort town that was the "Talk of the Western World." For more than 120 years, their vision has sustained Coronado, the Crown City.

One

CORONADO'S EARLY YEARS

On December 10, 1885, Elisha Babcock and Hampton Story transported Chinese laborers to Coronado on a barge towed behind Story's boat, *Della*. The barge also carried tents and camping gear for the laborers who would begin work clearing brush on Coronado. The men cleared brush during the day and burned the piles of debris at night, filling the air with smoke. From San Diego, little fires could be seen dotting the peninsula across the bay.

At the beginning of the new year, development was full-steam ahead on Coronado. A mechanic's lien was filed between George Marston and the Coronado Beach Company binding each to pay half the cost to pave Orange Avenue. By June 11, 1887, more than half of all lots on Coronado had been sold. The beach was proclaimed a moral community, and a prohibition clause was included on every deed sold. The *Coronado Evening Mercury* published the details of everyday life on the peninsula. As homes were built, the Coronado Beach Company gave residents marguerite daisies to use to grow borders around their properties.

Discussions of Coronado segregating from San Diego first began in the spring of 1888, and on June 3, 1890, an election was held to decide whether Coronado should separate. A majority of voters in both Coronado and San Diego was needed to carry the vote. The proposal was voted through, and on December 9, 1890, Coronado was officially incorporated. A board of trustees governed.

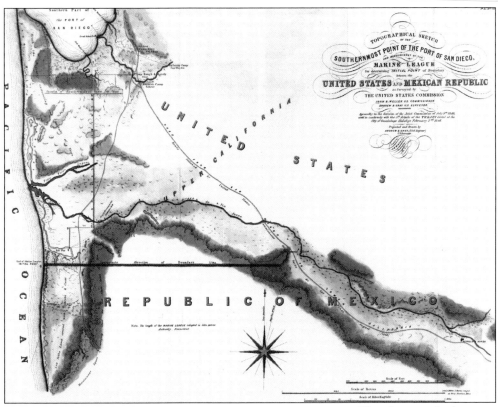

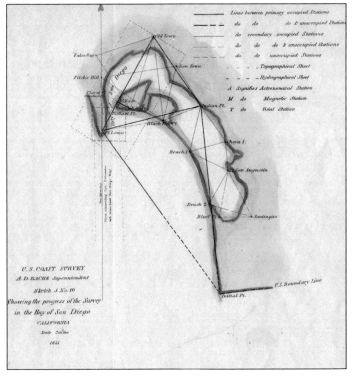

The photograph above shows a topographical sketch from 1849 of the southernmost point of the Port of San Diego and the defining boundary between the United States and Mexico. Note that the Coronado peninsula does not appear on this map. California was ceded to the United States after the Mexican-American War and was admitted to the Union on September 9, 1850, becoming the 31st state. In the picture at left, a U.S. coast survey was charted in 1851 showing the progress of San Diego Bay and Coronado's North and South Islands. (Both, CPL.)

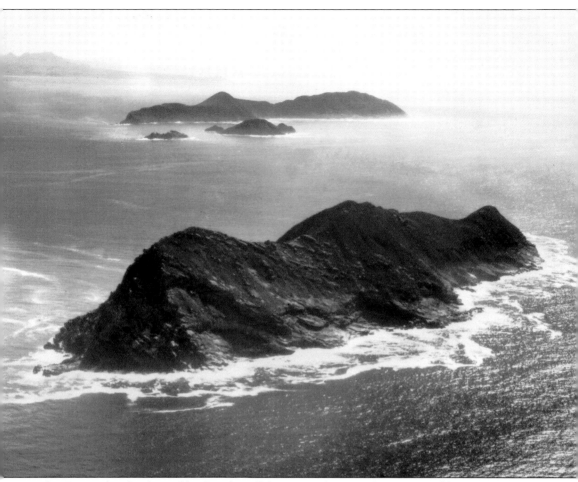

The Coronado Islands, visible 17 miles off the coast of Coronado, are owned by Mexico. The land mass consists of three islands and one rock that looks like a small island. In the 1800s, land speculators found the islands to be rich in animal and mineral resources. Day trips from the Hotel del Coronado to the islands introduced visitors to nature in its purest form. Guests could hike to elevated areas on the islands where gulls, cormorants, and pelicans nested, or explore the shore where sea lion and elephant seal rookeries were located. A quarry on one of the islands provided good foundation stone for construction purposes, and there was even a claim that gold was found on the islands. An expensive hotel and casino catering to affluent San Diegans and Hollywood elite was built on one of the islands in the 1930s, though it lasted only a few years before the Mexican government declared gambling illegal. Eventually the Mexican government forbade visitors to set foot on any of the islands. (SDHC.)

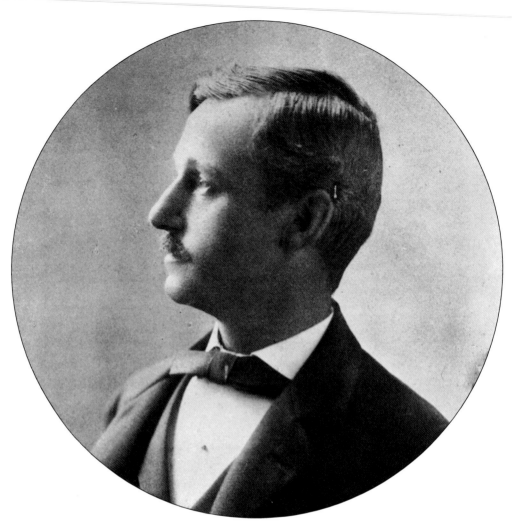

Elisha Spurr Babcock Jr., 1848–1922, a native of Evansville, Indiana, was an entrepreneur who came from humble means. He joined the U.S. Army as a young man and by the age of 23 had become a general freight agent of the Evansville and Terre Haute Railroad. He later became president of the Cumberland Telephone Company, then served as president of the Great Southern Telegraph Company. Babcock's health began to decline, and he was urged to winter in warmer climes, so he settled in San Diego in 1883. The city also proved to be a great location for his love of hunting and fishing. He was a frequent visitor to the North Island area of the Coronado peninsula to hunt quail and rabbits. It was these hunting expeditions that sparked the idea that later evolved into the development of Coronado Beach. (SDHC.)

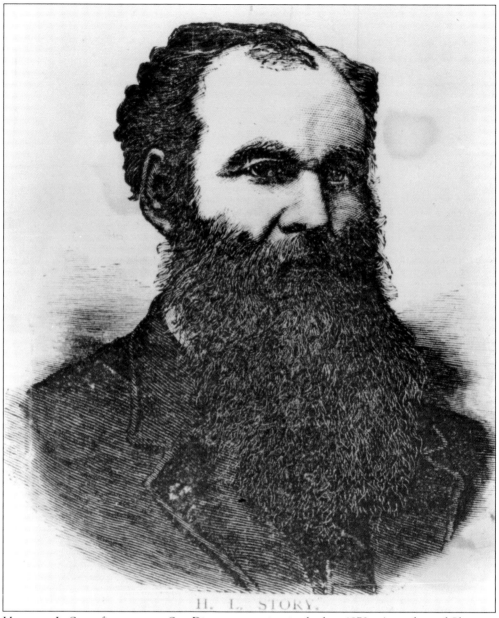

H. L. STORY.

Hampton L. Story first came to San Diego to vacation in the late 1870s. A resident of Chicago, he cofounded the Story and Clark Piano Company. By 1885, he had decided to retire, and he and his wife, Della, relocated to San Diego, buying a little farm in Chollas Valley, where present-day Highways 5 and 15 intersect, and a home in downtown San Diego near the intersection of First and A Avenues. Story bought a steam launch that he named after his wife. The Storys quickly became part of San Diego high society, throwing lavish parties and becoming well connected in their new city. Story's love of hunting and fishing was his link to Babcock. (SDHC.)

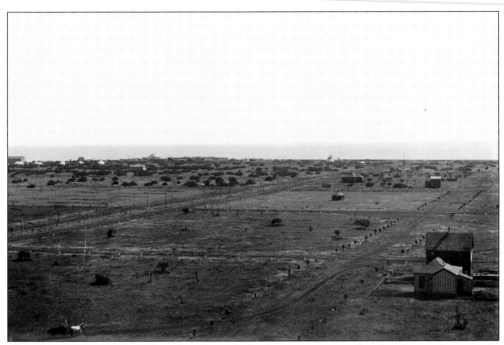

This photograph of Coronado, taken from the highest vantage on the island, provides a south-southwest view toward the ocean. Spanish bayonet (more commonly known as yucca), sumac, dwarf mahogany (probably manzanita), and other native plants grew wild. In the springtime, wildflowers bloomed on the vacant lots around the beach. (SDHC.)

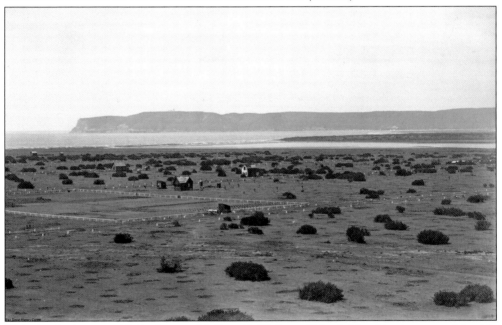

This view looks toward Point Loma with Spanish Bight and North Island in the upper right side of the picture. Streets were laid while brush was still being cleared off the land. The fenced area, owned by the Coronado Beach Company, grew fresh fruits and vegetables for use in the Hotel del Coronado's kitchen. (SDHC.)

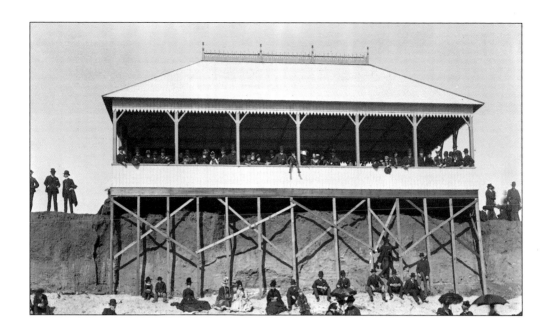

Babcock and Story built a large pavilion at the site of their proposed hotel that allowed visitors to view the scenery in comfort. The west side of the pavilion was outfitted with windows for protection from the breeze. A railroad track was designed to connect the ferry landing to the hotel site, and visitors arrived in droves to oversee the project, take tours of the construction layout, or simply picnic by the beach. The bluff's edge was eventually graded to a more gradual slope toward the water. The view of the ocean is not much different today than it was in 1886. (Above, SDHC; below, LHC.)

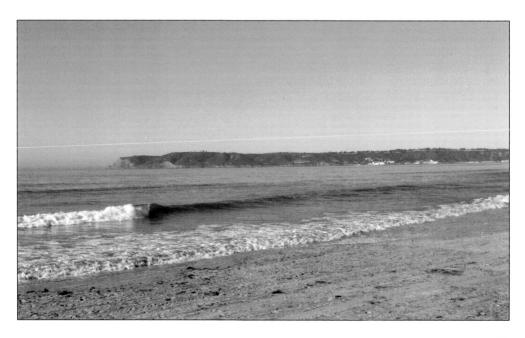

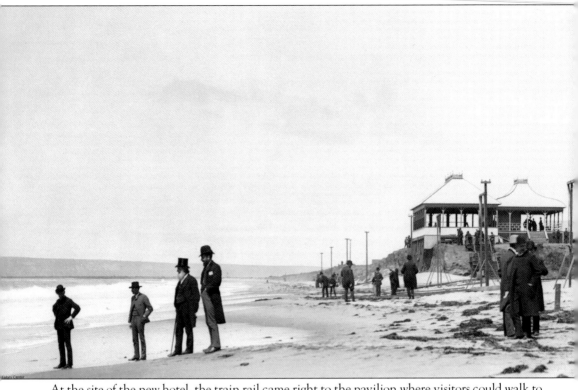

At the site of the new hotel, the train rail came right to the pavilion where visitors could walk to the water's edge. The Coronado Beach Company invited distinguished guests to a large reception at the pavilion in September 1886. The railroad along Orange Avenue had been finished months before and was ready for the hundreds of people who attended. They could not help but be dazzled by a beautifully lit pavilion on a September evening as they danced to orchestra music next to the ocean, under a full moon. The men standing to the left side on the beach in this picture are said to be, from left to right, Elisha Babcock, Harry Titus, Alonzo Horton, and Hampton Story. (SDHC.)

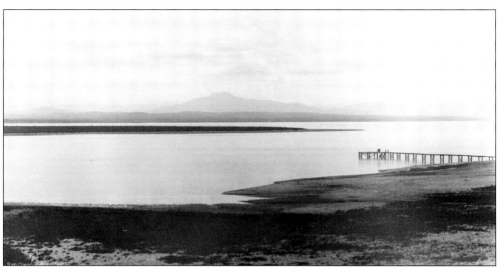

This c. 1886 photograph shows the pier before the construction of a boathouse along Glorietta Bay, which was dredged in 1887 to make way for bigger boats. The dredging also filled in the shoreline to widen the area between the ocean and the bay and to straighten out the shoreline for the purpose of development. (SDHC.)

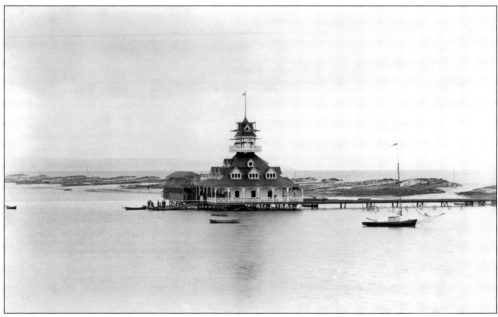

Built in the same Victorian style as the future hotel, the boathouse, Coronado's oldest landmark, was completed in July 1887. Skilled laborers were hard to find during the building boom in San Diego, and it is believed that the boathouse's construction provided training for workers hired to build the hotel. In 1968, the boathouse was moved 70 feet closer to the shoreline to its present location. (SDHC.)

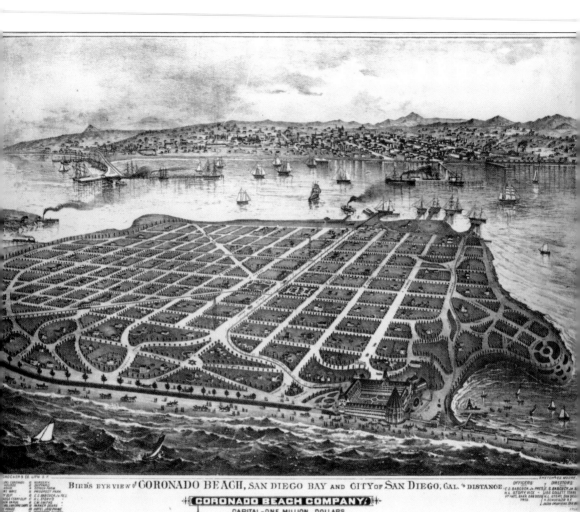

This map, created by the Coronado Beach Company, was sketched by E. S. Moore of Crocker and Company, lithographers in San Francisco. It was first published in 1886. The map offers a bird's-eye view of the land, showing tree-lined streets and horse buggies on the beach. City blocks in the center grid measured 300 by 500 feet, surrounded by irregularly shaped blocks on the perimeter. The streets in the grid section were numbered and lettered for ease of navigation. The outer streets were named for various people, most notably Adella Avenue named after Della Story and Isabella Avenue named after Isabel Babcock, the wives of Coronado's founders. More than 100,000 copies of the map were distributed around the United States and Canada. (SDHC.)

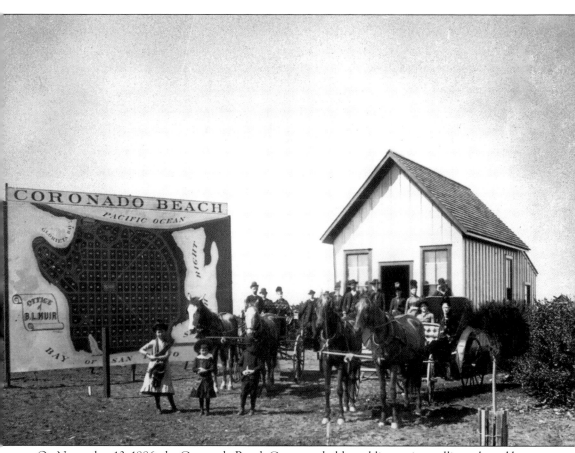

On November 13, 1886, the Coronado Beach Company held a public auction, selling selected lots on Coronado Beach. The ferry made trips across the bay every 30 minutes to accommodate the crowds. More than 6,000 people came over from San Diego to be part of the activities. An article written in the *San Diego Union* the day after the event stated that after visitors got off the ferry they were "thence whirled by steam-cars from bay shore to sea shore along an avenue lined with oranges trees and spraying fountains." A large tent by the beach was erected for the auction, and a free lunch of coffee and sandwiches was served. Bidding began at 11:00 a.m., and by the end of the day 350 lots had sold for a total of $110,000. Maj. Levi Chase, the lawyer who negotiated the purchase of the peninsula for Babcock and Story, bought the first oceanfront lot. (SDHC.)

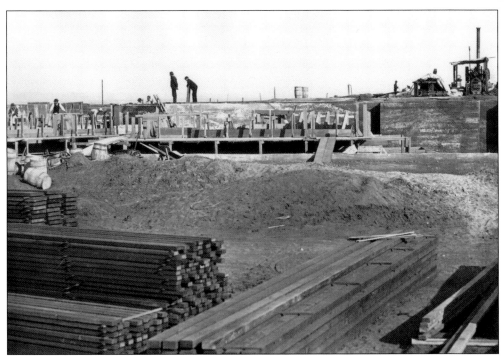

The foundation of the new Hotel del Coronado was 12 feet high, according to the *San Diego Union*, and contained 14,000 barrels of cement, several tons of sand, and 250,000 tons of broken stone. The hotel's foundation ran a total of 2,308 linear feet. Hampton Story (left) and Elisha Babcock are seen here inspecting the foundation. (SDHC.)

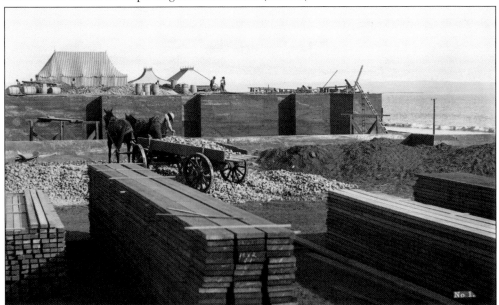

Millions of feet of lumber were used for the construction of the hotel. Two hundred and fifty men were employed in various capacities of construction. The Reid brothers, architects, employed seven men who worked exclusively on drafting plans. To save time, no final plans were drawn for the hotel; construction was supervised from simple drawings and drafts. (SDHC.)

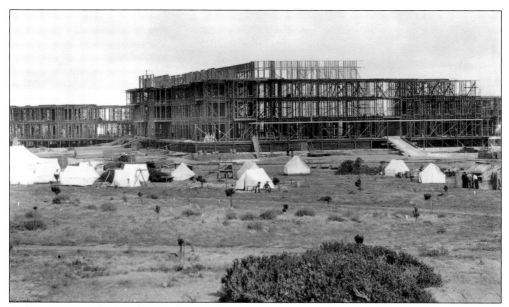

A dormitory was built to house the construction workers, but it quickly filled up. Looking at the northwest side of the hotel, tents in the foreground provided an overflow encampment for workers. Light masts were installed allowing for two work shifts: 11-hour-long day shifts and 11-hour-long night shifts. (SDHC.)

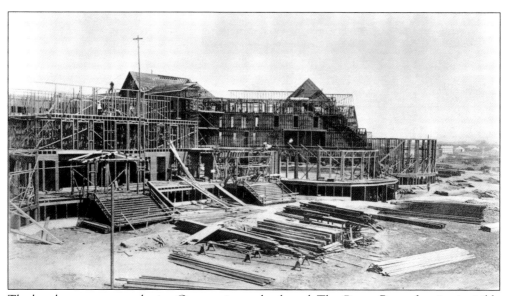

The hotel was constructed using Oregon pine and redwood. The Crown Room framing is visible on the right. There were two entrances on the east side of the hotel, one closer to the ocean for women so they might "freshen up" after being outside, the other for men with tiled floors so they could drop their fish or game for hotel staff to clean. (SDHC.)

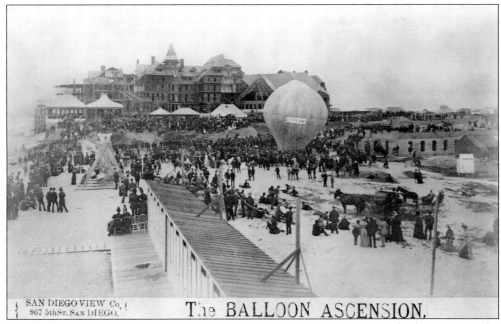

The BALLOON ASCENSION.

This photograph, taken October 2, 1887, depicts a balloon ascension, which was quite the event in the late 1800s. Prof. Emiel de Melville, called "The World's Greatest Aeronaut in his Mammoth Airship," was to pilot the balloon, *City of Tia Juana*, according to an advertisement in the *Coronado Evening Mercury*. All were invited, at no charge, to watch the balloon rise over the crowd. (SDHC.)

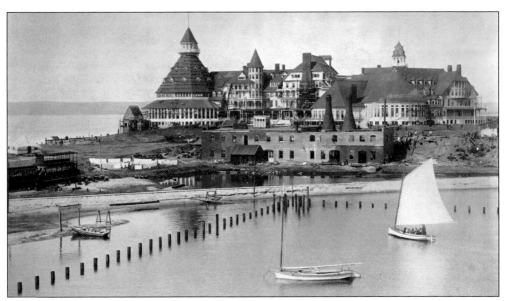

As hotel construction progressed, visitors came through daily on tours. Because the building contained so much flammable material, "No Smoking" signs were posted at all entrances and fireproof paint was used inside and out. The pilings (lower left) formed the perimeter for a dredging project in Glorietta Bay, which aimed to widen the strip between the ocean and the bay. (SDHC.)

22

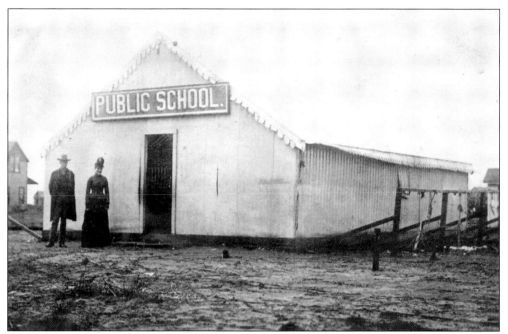

With the development of Coronado came families and their children. The first public school building was a tent erected at Seventh Street and D Avenue. In January 1887, school officially opened; it concluded for the summer with 34 students. In the fall, enrollment increased to 75 children, necessitating a second, temporary building. By 1892, close to 250 children were enrolled. (CPL.)

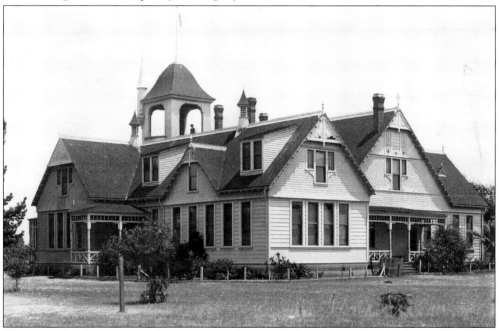

The school bond election in July 1887 won with a resounding eight votes. The third public school building, constructed at a cost of $17,000, was completed in early 1888. Facing Sixth Street between E and F Avenues, the structure contained eight classrooms, 240 desks, and a library on the first floor. (CPL.)

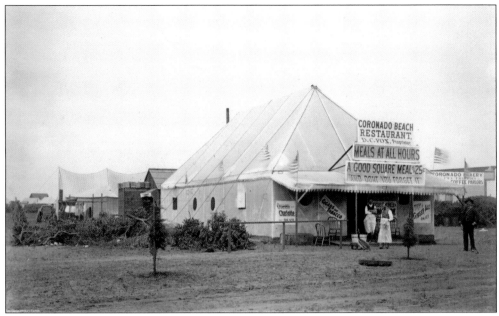

D. C. Fox owned one of two restaurants in early Coronado, located in the vicinity of the El Cordova Hotel. He also holds the distinction of opening the first library at Coronado Beach, known as the Reading Room. Lit by electricity, it provided a nice respite for many workers of the beach company. (SDHC.)

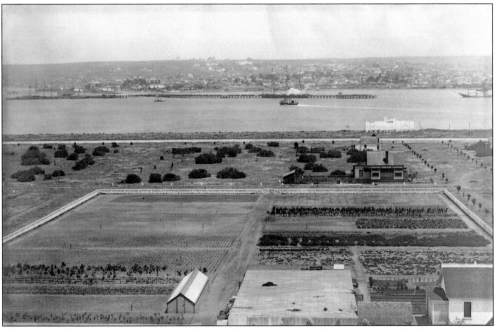

There were three nurseries at the beach. The Beach Company Nursery, later called the Botanical Gardens, grew a variety of plants and featured a rose house made entirely of glass. Solon and Anne Blaisdell and Kate Sessions opened a subsidiary of the San Diego Nursery. Sessions also supervised the landscaping and gardens at the Hotel del Coronado. (SDHC.)

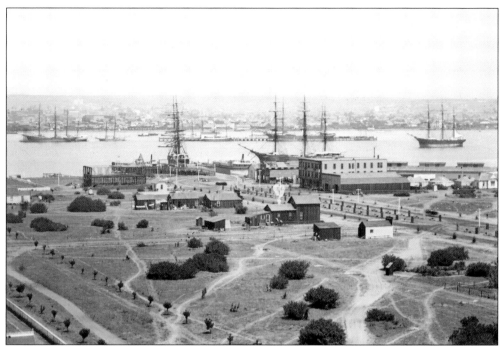

Looking toward San Diego Bay, this photograph taken around 1887 shows businesses building near the wharf. By the following year, a ferry house was completed. City blocks began to take shape as trees were planted along the streets, but most of the beach was still open and people crossed the empty lots without regard for boundary markings. (SDHC.)

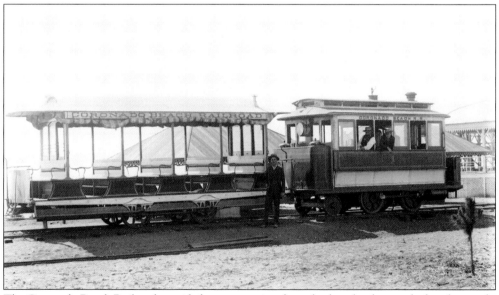

The Coronado Beach Railroad provided transportation from the ferry landing to the hotel grounds. This 50-seat excursion car was pulled by a steam engine. Shipped from Rochester, New York, this streetcar was the same type used at Coney Island. The car could be opened to the fresh breeze or closed up in a matter of moments, maximizing comfort for the riders. (SDHC.)

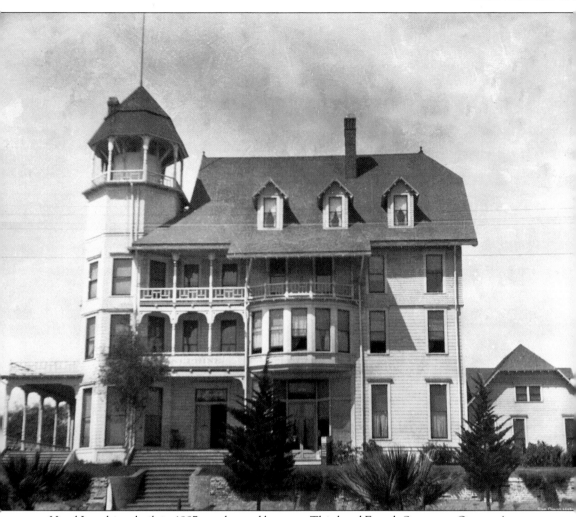

Hotel Josephine, built in 1887, was located between Third and Fourth Streets on Orange Avenue. The hotel, which was designed by the famed Reid brothers, was built in Eastlake style with a cut-shingle finish above the second story. Built at a cost of $30,000, the hotel boasted 64 rooms and was three stories high with a fourth half-story for servants' quarters. The section of road on this block of Orange Avenue was graded due to a rise in the land between Third and Fourth Streets that runs northwest to southeast across Coronado. The Hotel Josephine was built on top of this area with a retaining wall in place across the front. After Coronado was incorporated as a city in 1890, the new city's board of trustees held its first meetings here. Eventually the hotel was sold and renamed the Hotel Iturbide. The San Diego Army and Navy Academy was formed here in 1910 but closed after a few years. The building was torn down in 1915. (SDHC.)

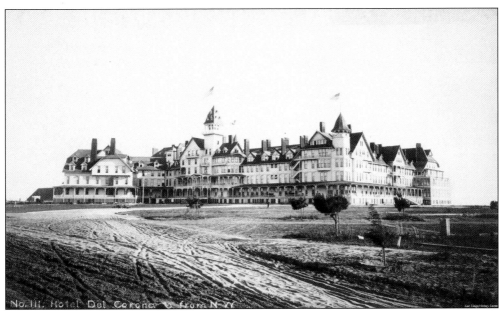

The Hotel del Coronado was the first hotel in the world to have electric lighting throughout. A bit experimental, the electric wiring ran inside gas lines, so if the electricity did not work, it would be possible to pipe gas to the rooms. The wiring was successful and the electric steam plant was so powerful that all of Coronado was supplied with power until 1922. The hotel is said to have cost $600,000 to build and another $400,000 to furnish. The Hotel del Coronado was truly a wonder to behold. (SDHC.)

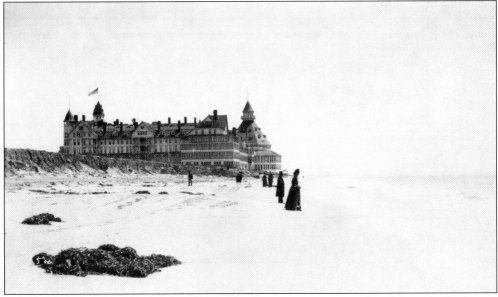

Hotel del Coronado was marketed as a health resort. People diagnosed with bronchial ailments such as tuberculosis, asthma, and hay fever, as well as rheumatism and other ailments of the day, came to San Diego for temperate weather, unspoiled land, and fresh ocean breezes. Enjoying sunshine on the beach may have been just what the doctor ordered. (SDHC.)

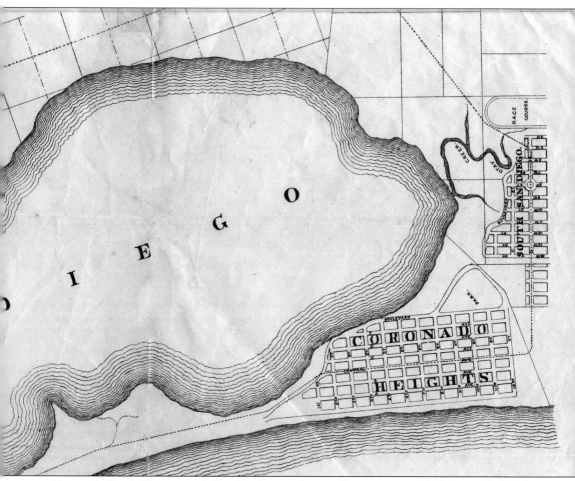

Coronado Beach Company tried to develop another small community called Coronado Heights, located at the southern end of the strand, just south of the present-day Coronado Cays. Ten blocks long and seven blocks wide, advertisements called it the "Pasadena of San Diego" and a "Charming Suburb of Coronado Beach." The layout was similar to Coronado Beach in regard to block sizes, wide streets, and landscaping. H. L. Story personally supervised the tree planting, some of which still grow there today. There was promise of a hotel at the north end, resulting in lots selling briskly, but an economic depression settled in and the project never got off the ground. Most buyers had only made a minimal payment and later walked away from the properties. Today the property is only accessible to U.S. Navy personnel who use the land for training purposes. (SDHC.)

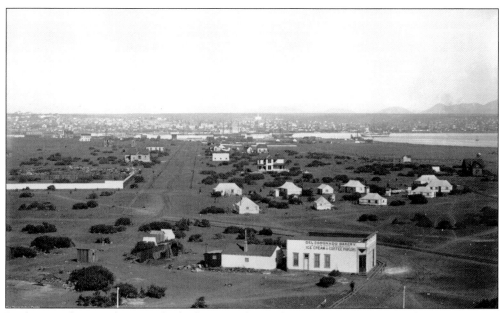

In this aerial view of Coronado, looking northeast down A Avenue, the blocks closest to the hotel construction are starting to fill up with dwellings. Due to the shortage of materials and labor, large tents were used as temporary housing until homes could be built. The fence line of an ostrich farm is visible on the left. (SDHC.)

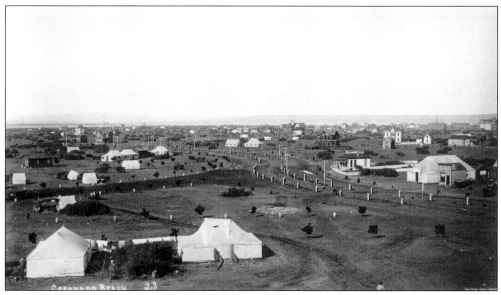

This view looking north from the Hotel del Coronado focuses on what is now the intersection of Orange and B Avenues. A chicken ranch was started off to the left near the dormitory building. It was home to 500 chickens that were a plentiful source of eggs for hotel guests. (SDHC)

29

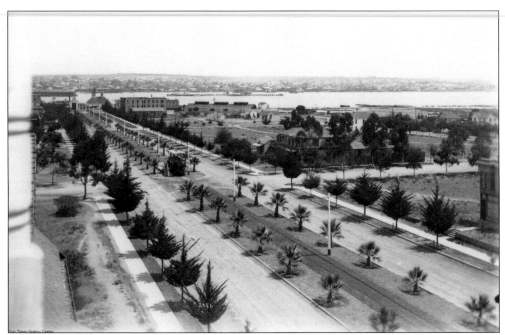

This view looks northeast down Orange Avenue toward the ferry landing. Charles Orcutt, a neighbor to H. L. Story's ranch in Chollas Valley, supervised the systematic planting of trees on Coronado. The trees were supplied from Orcutt's nursery in Chollas Valley. Many trees still living in Coronado today date back to those early years. (1906 Lodge.)

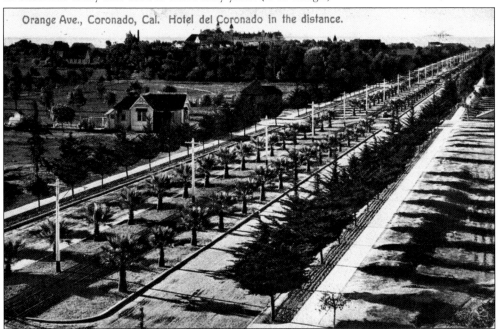

Looking southwest, the hotel can be seen in the distance. Originally, orange trees were planted down Orange Avenue, but the combination of rabbits and wind proved to be too much for the trees to withstand. Within a few years, palm and cypress trees replaced the orange trees, but Coronado's main street retained its citrusy name. (SDHC.)

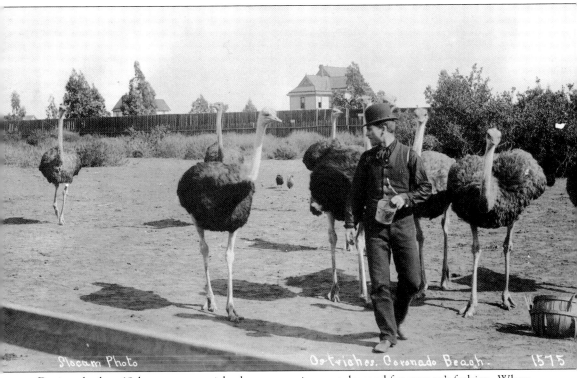

Slocum Photo   Ostriches. Coronado Beach.   1575

During the late 19th century, ostrich plumes were in great demand for women's fashion. When the ostrich farm opened in Coronado in 1887, advertisements in the *Coronado Evening Mercury* touted the ostriches as "a rare opportunity to see birds of various sizes and ages." Ostriches are very strong, typically ill-tempered, and pack a vicious kick, so plucking feathers required great care. The *Coronado Evening Mercury* reported that when an ostrich got feisty the farm manager would run for safety into a clump of bushes until the bird would lose interest. On May 30, 1887, the *Coronado Evening Mercury* reported that, "Coronado has had the first newspaper, the first baby, the first wedding, the first ostriches, the first fire company, and another great event has come to pass—the first ostrich egg laid on the beach." About 1904, the ostrich farm was moved to Mission Hills, next to the Mission Cliff Gardens. (CPL.)

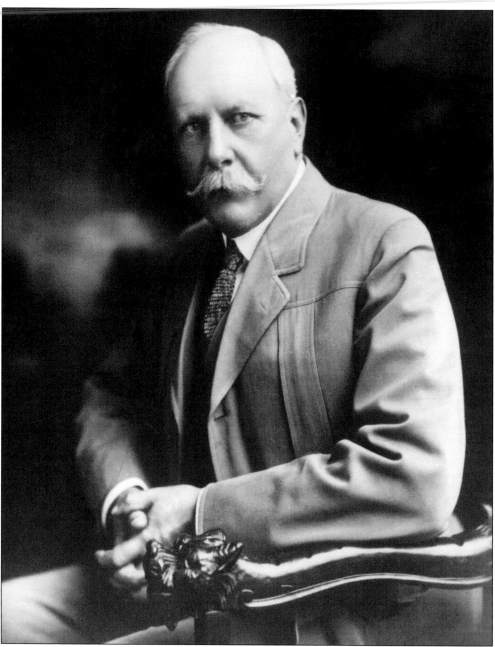

John Dietrich Spreckels was Coronado's patron saint. Although Spreckels was not part of the inception of Coronado, he played the largest role in Coronado's early history. By 1892, Spreckels filed articles of incorporation in the ownership of the Hotel del Coronado, North Island, and most of the Coronado beach property. Spreckels was the richest man in San Diego, allowing him to keep the Hotel del Coronado solvent and successful in addition to constructing a public library, two homes, and the Spreckels building on Orange Avenue. He had multiple holdings in San Diego, and at one point he paid 10 percent of all property taxes in San Diego. John D. Spreckels spent millions of dollars inspired by the potential of San Diego and Coronado, leaving a legacy of culture and quality of life for millions of people. (SDHC.)

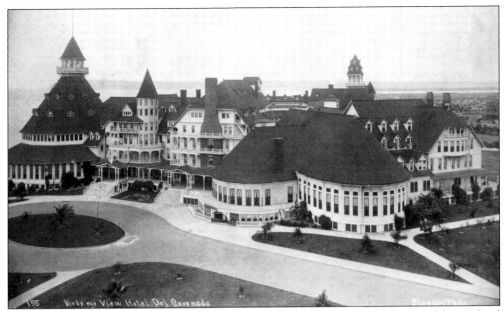

This view looking down at the Hotel del Coronado shows the different elevations of the roof and the spectacular architecture of the hotel. The highest point from ground to top measured 120 feet. A telescope was placed in the highest cupola for guests at the hotel to view Coronado and the surrounding areas. (SDHC.)

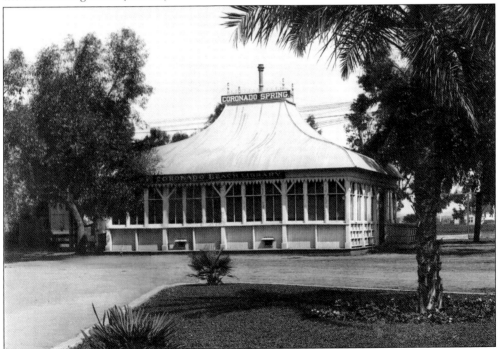

The Coronado Beach Public Library, pictured here around 1895, was housed in the original beachfront pavilion. Eventually moved across the street from the Hotel del Coronado, the library was called the "Spring House" because water was pumped to it for a few years under the guise of being therapeutic. (CPL.)

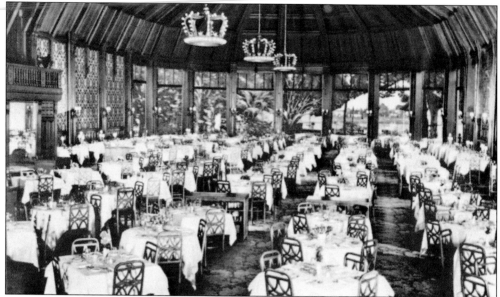

The Crown Room, the Hotel del Coronado's exquisite dining hall, is considered an architectural wonder. The crown-shaped light fixtures were designed by L. Frank Baum, famed author of *The Wonderful Wizard of Oz.* Baum vacationed in Coronado for years, first staying at the hotel, later renting a home on Star Park. He wrote three books in his Wizard of Oz series during visits to Coronado. (LHC.)

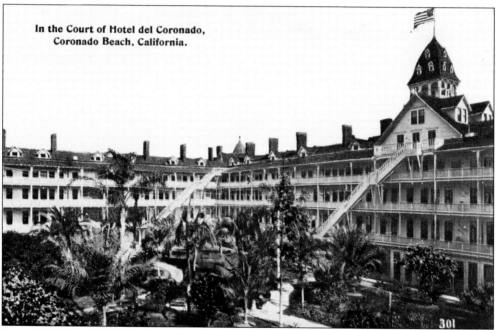

According to the *Coronado Evening Mercury*, "The interior courtyard plantings were to include everything of a tropical nature in the way of plants, trees and flowers." The courtyard measured 150 by 250 feet. Note the chimneys across the roof and the interior stairways that were removed in later years. Famed horticulturalist Kate Sessions was commissioned to supervise the plantings at Hotel del Coronado. (LHC.)

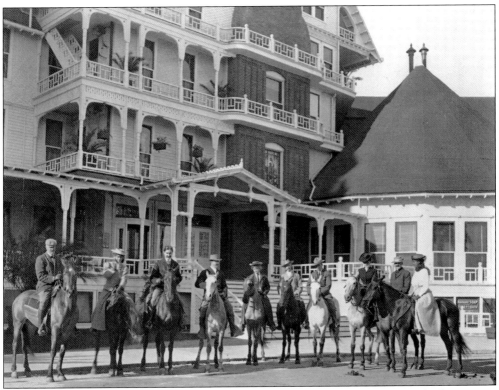

During the first years the hotel was open, guests had the option to participate in multiple activities on and around Coronado Beach. This group is preparing for a rabbit hunt on North Island. Entertainment available for guests included fishing trips, horseback riding, yachting, tennis, trap shooting, and archery, as well as a planted labyrinth and natural history museum. (SDHC.)

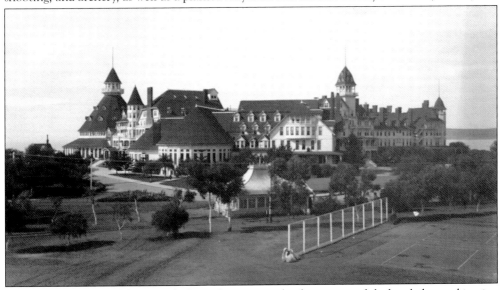

This view of the Hotel del Coronado shows the maturing landscape around the hotel, the combination train station and library, and tennis courts in the foreground. John D. Spreckels worked diligently to develop Coronado into a first-class town deserving of his first-class hotel. (CPL.)

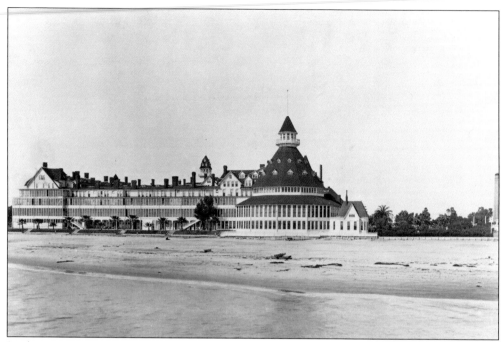

Looking at the Hotel del Coronado from the beach side in this c. 1900 image, the use of windows to bring light to every room in the hotel becomes very apparent. The hotel had 2,372 windows. The Grand Ballroom, featured prominently in this photograph, overlooks the Pacific Ocean. Early on, there was no substantial protection from high surf if a storm came through. (SDHC.)

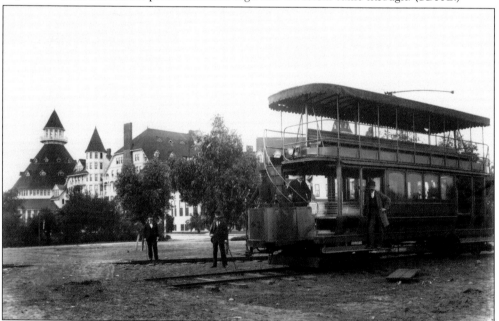

The railroad station across from the Hotel del Coronado was connected to the hotel by electric wire. A push button placed at the rail station would ring a bell in the hotel, announcing the arrival and departure of trains. This double-decker streetcar provided a stunning view of Coronado as it chugged across the peninsula. (SDHC.)

Two

Tent City

Coronado's Tent City was the brainchild of John D. Spreckels. He saw the need for a more affordable vacation spot for the masses. Tent City opened in June 1900 and stayed open until the beginning of September. It was an instant success. When Tent City opened, most tents rented for $4.50 a week. Extra amenities could be added for a fee, but even then accommodations were much more reasonable than the $3.50 a night it cost at the Hotel Del Coronado.

The electric railway ran down Main Street flanked by Glorietta Bay and the Pacific Ocean. Each year, the camping area became more popular, anticipated by visitors and the peninsula residents. Tent City had its own newspaper that reported on visitors in residence and listed a calendar of events. During the summer when visitors and residents mingled, lasting friendships were forged.

However, by 1939, Tent City was waning. Spreckels's heirs had sold the Hotel del Coronado a few years prior and the new owners may have been a contributing factor to the area's decline, but Coronado was also undergoing a hefty transformation as military presence increased, resulting in the ultimate demise of Tent City. A highway was routed through the center of the little vacation city, marking the end of a very special way of life for Coronado's guests and residents.

Originally known as Camp Coronado, the Spreckels Company advertised Tent City far and wide. A marketing postcard read, "As a seaside resort beyond question Coronado Tent City is the gem of the Pacific coast. The arrangements for the comfort and pleasure of the public have been planned and executed with boldness, wisdom and liberality." The Tent City Band traveled on a private railcar around Southern California for the specific purpose of advertising Camp Coronado. (1906 Lodge.)

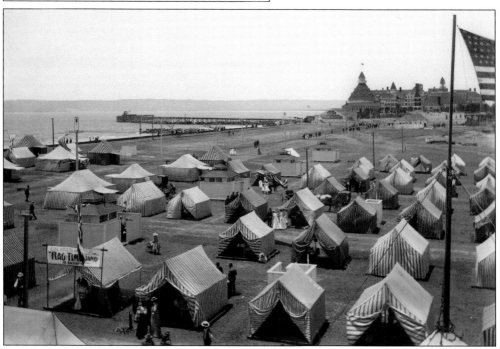

Tent City opened in 1900 with 100 tents custom-ordered from the Swanfeldt Tent Company of Los Angeles. The first tents were produced using white or red- and white-striped canvas. Arthur Swanfeldt supervised the building of the camp during the first year. The tents were dismantled in the fall, but the wooden floors were kept in place through the winter. (SDHC.)

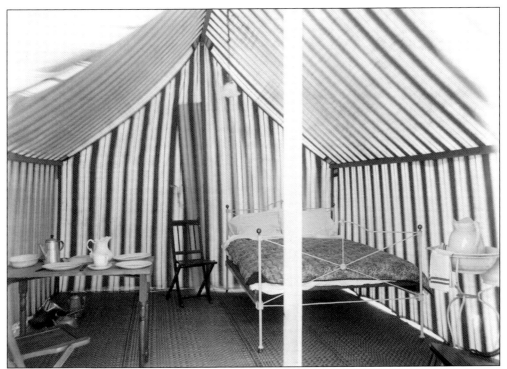

Tent City provided the basic comforts of home. The tents had wooden floors, beds, a dresser, chair, and washstand. For an added fee, a small tent with a stove and cooking utensils could be connected to the main tent. (SDHC.)

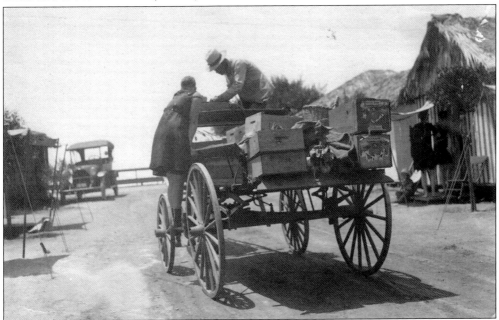

A vegetable cart was available to guests of Tent City courtesy of Chinese vendors who sold produce grown in little plots they leased from the Spreckles Company on North Island. Other amenities available to campers could be bought in the general store. (CHA.)

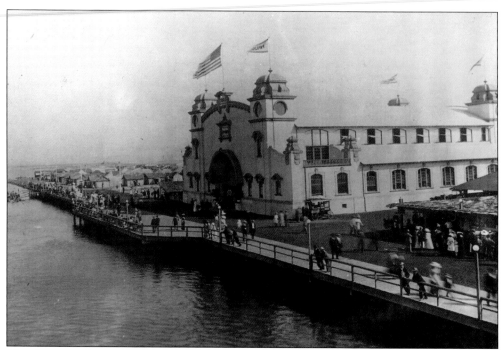

The dance pavilion at Tent City was the largest pavilion on the West Coast, hosting functions that were attended by hundreds. The building also doubled as a bowling alley and skating rink. It was torn down in 1939 when Tent City permanently closed. (1906 Lodge.)

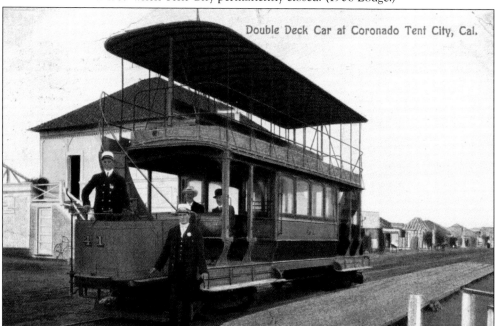

Double Deck Car at Coronado Tent City, Cal.

This double-decker car ran up and down Main Street in Tent City. The Orange Avenue electric line was extended down the hill from the Hotel del Coronado station to a connecting junction that hooked into the Belt Line, providing complete rail transportation through Coronado. (1906 Lodge.)

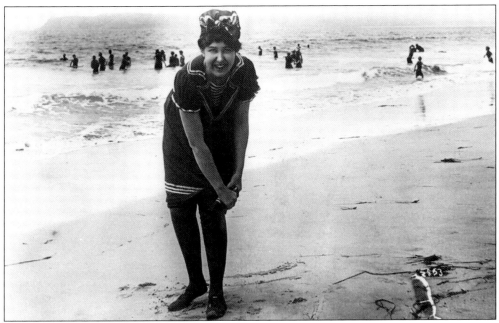

Tent City supplied the needs of beachgoers by offering bathing suits, caps, and stockings for rent. Women wore a full suit and stockings to keep their bodies covered up. When wet, the weight of their bathing clothes kept women from venturing too far in the water. Men's swimwear was typically a swimming or rowing leotard with much less coverage than women's suits. In 1919, an ordinance was passed, making it a violation for anyone over the age of 12 to wear a bathing suit on the streets of Coronado city limits without being covered by a wrap or robe. Women at the Hotel del Coronado mocked this ordinance by playing tennis in their bathing suits, to the delight of spectators. (Both, SDHC.)

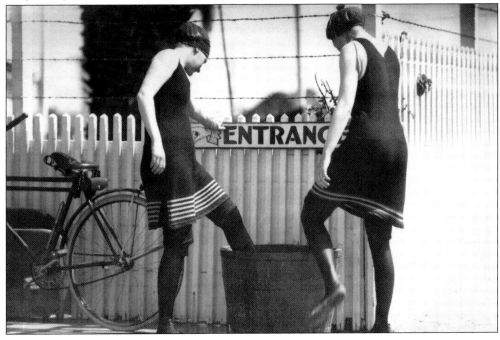

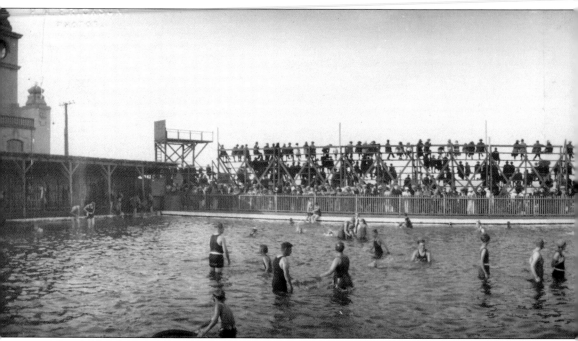

The children's swimming tank was built with a gradual drop-off and was no deeper than 3 feet. A sandy bottom was added to the tank in 1902. It was located next to the dance pavilion and behind the bleachers facing Glorietta Bay where spectators could watch diving competitions while keeping

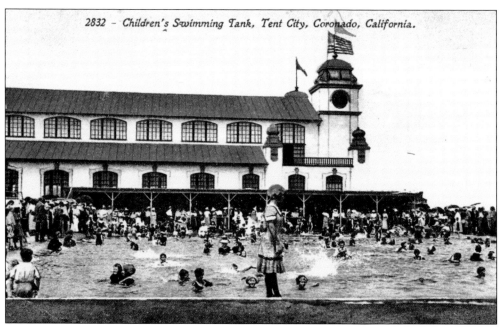

2832 – Children's Swimming Tank, Tent City, Coronado, California.

Coronado was heaven to children visiting Tent City. For 78¢, swimmers could rent a bathing suit for a week and spend hours in a warm saltwater pool while parents watched from the bleachers above. The dance pavilion next door also served as a skating rink and bowling alley, providing activities for all ages. (LHC.)

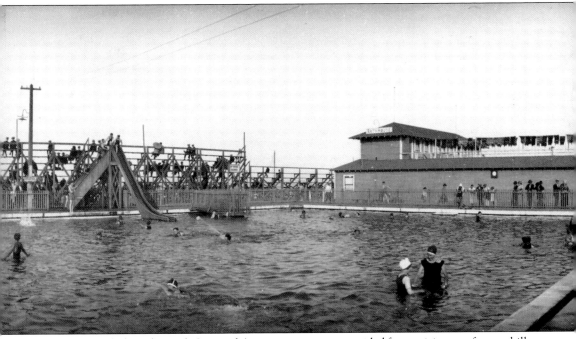

an eye on their kids in the pool. Coronado's water sports were provided for participants of every skill level. From the children's swimming tank to the ocean waters where ropes extended from the shore for people to grasp when they ventured into the surf, safety was always a concern. (CPL.)

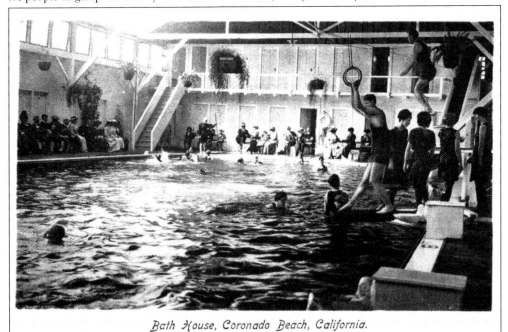

Bath House, Coronado Beach, California.

The bathhouse, also known as the saltwater plunge, was located on the ocean side of Tent City. The therapeutic qualities of saltwater were highly regarded at the time. The bathhouse contained warm and cold saltwater plunge baths, with the water being replaced three times a day. The *Tent City News* reported, "L. E. Wallis gives swimming lessons at Hotel Bath House." (1906 Lodge.)

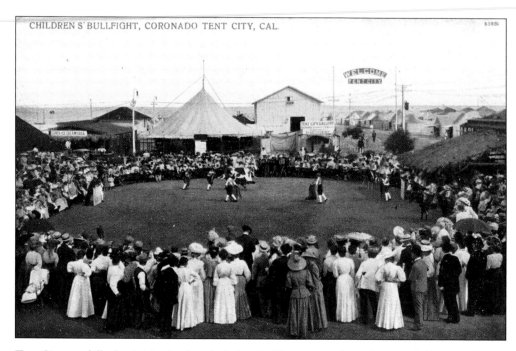

CHILDREN'S BULLFIGHT, CORONADO TENT CITY, CAL.

Tent City was full of activities for the whole family. The picture above shows a children's bullfight. Below, children are participating in a watermelon-eating contest. Children could ride burros on the beach and meet baby monkeys and sea lions at the petting zoo. Families could catch shows at the outdoor theater in the evenings. A carousel was brought to Tent City sometime after 1910. In 1915, it was moved to Balboa Park for the Panama-California Exposition but returned to Tent City for nearly seven more years. The carousel is now permanently placed in Balboa Park, next to the entrance of the San Diego Zoo. (Both, 1906 Lodge.)

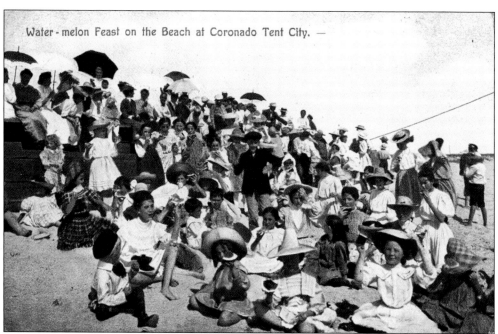

Water-melon Feast on the Beach at Coronado Tent City. —

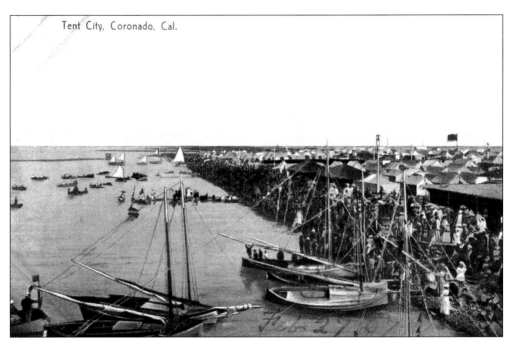

Tent City, Coronado, Cal.

Tent City published its own newspaper and reported on the various activities available to visitors, as well as the comings and goings of tenants during the summer. The camp exceeded all expectations presuming its popularity. A small police force was finally put in place when holidays proved to push the crowds to extremes and behavior went awry, but for the most part, the environment was very family friendly. Businesses vied heavily for a presence in Tent City and offered a wide variety of services and goods. Open-air concerts were performed every evening, vaudeville acts were presented, and sightseeing tours were offered in neighboring San Diego. (Above, 1906 Lodge; below, LHC.)

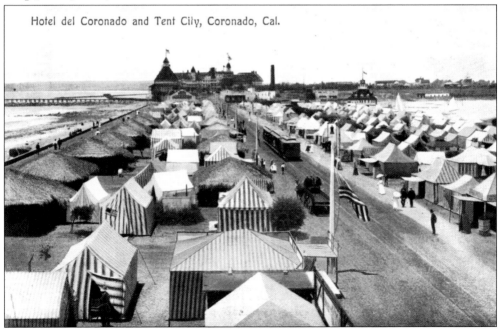

Hotel del Coronado and Tent City, Coronado, Cal.

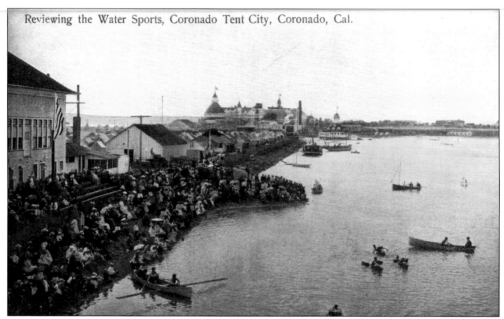

Sailboats and canoes were rented at the boathouse, swimming matches and diving competitions were viewed from the bleachers overlooking Glorietta Bay, and fishing events took place from the dock. In this photograph, taken from the Silvergate party boat, a typical weekend crowd in Tent City is illustrated. (1906 Lodge.)

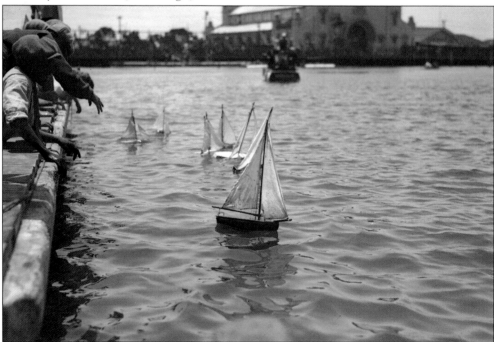

In this picture, model sailboat racing enthusiasts launch their boats from a floating dock in Glorietta Bay. Children came from San Diego and beyond to compete in these model sailboat regattas. The dance pavilion is seen in the background (top right) with the observation bleachers next to it (top left). (SDHC.)

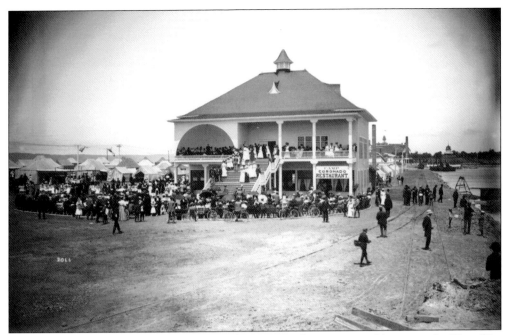

The Camp Coronado Restaurant was a gathering spot for visitors and home to the Tent City Band. Entertainment at Tent City became a popular draw for visitors, and in 1901, entertainment managers were hired to organize all of the musicians and entertainers who were hired at Tent City for either single performances or seasonal jobs. (SDHC.)

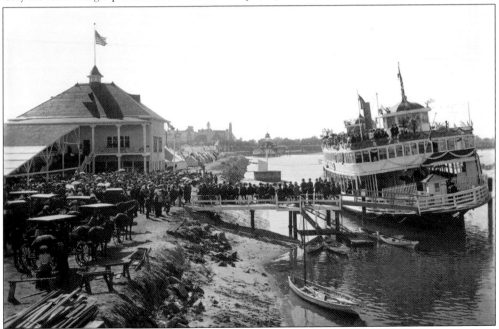

Adjacent to the café was the casino, formerly the *Silvergate* ferry. Launched April 1, 1888, the ferry was doomed from the beginning. It was poorly designed, too big and unwieldy, and it routinely damaged docks on both sides of the bay. Decommissioned after two years, the ferry found a new life at Tent City until 1910 and later as a clubhouse for the San Diego Yacht Club. (SDHC.)

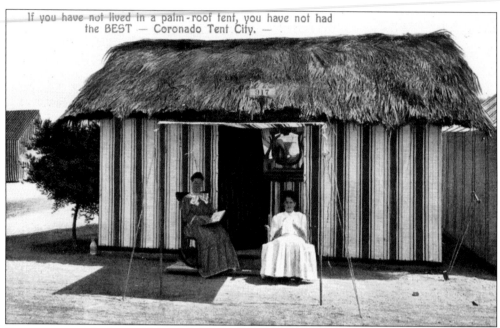

If you have not lived in a palm-roof tent, you have not had the BEST — Coronado Tent City. —

Two women watch the world go by from their tent in this photograph taken around 1910. Main Street, Ocean Front, and Bay Front were the three roads that ran parallel to each other in Tent City. Numbered streets intersected these roads, creating a small grid pattern similar to that in the city of Coronado. For the convenience of campers, barrels of water were stationed at each street corner to provide hydration on hot summer days. (1906 Lodge.)

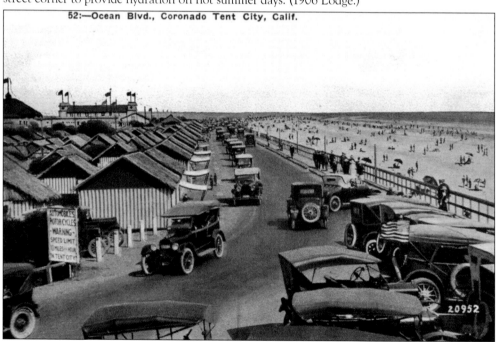

52:—Ocean Blvd., Coronado Tent City, Calif.

Cars eventually became a part of the perimeter roads at Tent City. The speed limit for cars and bicycles was 10 miles per hour, but even with that slow speed, Tent City could probably claim the first traffic jams on Coronado. (1906 Lodge.)

Three

CORONADO FERRIES

The Coronado ferries are an important footnote in the peninsula's history. Babies were born on the ferry. Kids could take a bike and have a great day of adventure across the bay in San Diego. Leaving Coronado meant entering the bigger and busier life on the San Diego side. Coming back to Coronado meant breathing a little easier. A typical ferry ride was about 10 minutes long each way, and it gave patrons the chance to relax, mingle, and reflect upon the natural wonder and beauty of the bay area.

In addition to the ferry service between San Diego and Coronado, ferries ran between San Diego and the northern part of the peninsula, North Island, for the convenience of military commuters. For a brief time in the 1880s, ferries ran between San Diego and Roseville on Point Loma, and a stern-wheel steamer ran down to the South Bay, presumably for residents at Coronado Heights and the Oneonta sections of San Diego. The unveiling of the Coronado-San Diego Bridge on August 3, 1969, marked the end of the leisurely ferries and the end of a traditional aspect of life on Coronado. The last five ferryboats that plied the waters of the San Diego Bay were sold off and met very different fates. Only two of the five are still afloat; the *Crown City* operates at Martha's Vineyard and the *San Diego* has been abandoned and is deteriorating by the shore on the Sacramento River. A salvaged ticket booth placed in Centennial Park at Orange Avenue and First Street rests as a reminder of the nostalgic ferry days of Coronado.

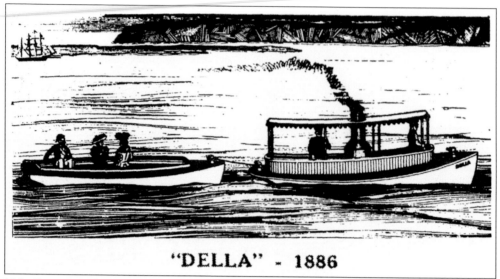

"DELLA" - 1886

H. L. Story owned Coronado's first ferry, *Della*, a 21-foot steam yacht. Named for his wife, Adella, the ferry was operated as a towboat for the Coronado Beach Company and helped transport Chinese laborers to the peninsula. It was later used to move passengers and supplies across the bay. *Della* sunk in 1887 when it crossed too closely ahead of a barkentine and capsized. (LHC.)

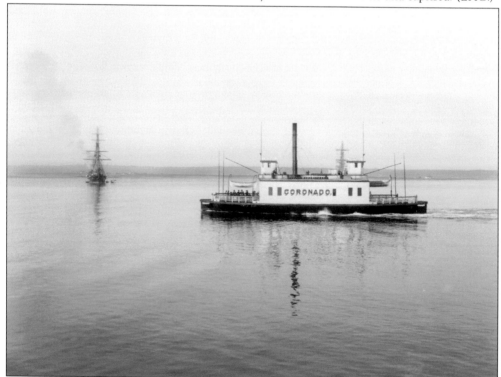

On April 16, 1886, Babcock and Story filed articles of incorporation for the San Diego and Coronado Ferry Company, retaining the sole right to provide transportation from San Diego to Coronado. The new ferry was ordered in San Francisco in March 1886. The *Coronado*, which cost $15,000, was formally commissioned and put into service on August 19, 1886. (SDHC.)

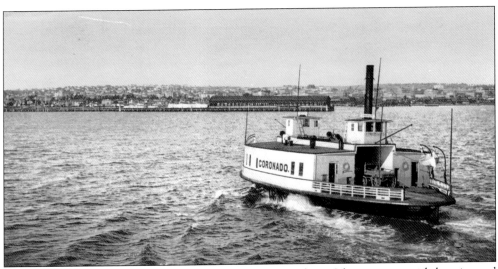

The *Coronado*, measuring 100 feet long, could accommodate 13 horse teams with buggies and 600 people. In addition to ferrying responsibilities, the *Coronado* was used to transport materials and workers during construction of the Hotel Del Coronado. A round-trip on Sunday cost 25¢. (CPL.)

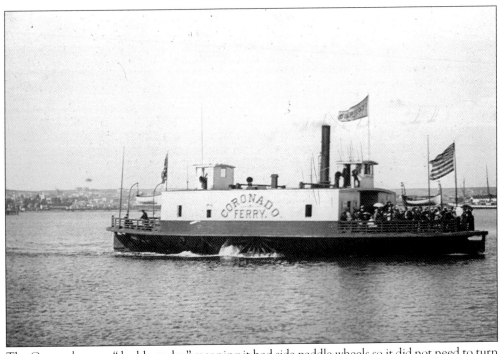

The *Coronado* was a "double-ender," meaning it had side paddle wheels so it did not need to turn around at each side of the bay. The *Coronado* operated in the San Diego Bay from 1886 until 1922 when it was sold to a Hollywood film company and blown up for a movie. (CPL.)

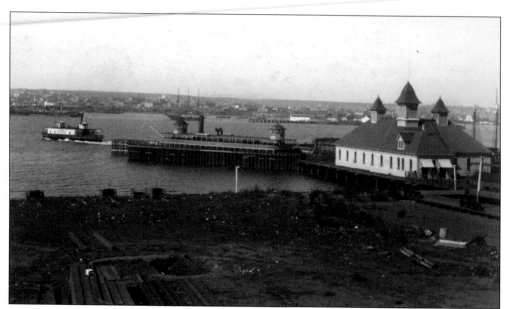

The ferry landing building (right) was constructed in 1888. The architects who designed the building also designed Coronado's first "real" schoolhouse and other notable structures in San Diego. The ferry house featured turrets, stained glass windows, a ticket office, and water closets for men and women, costing $7,000 to build. Synchronized electric clocks were installed at the ferry house, the company's offices, and the Hotel del Coronado. (CPL.)

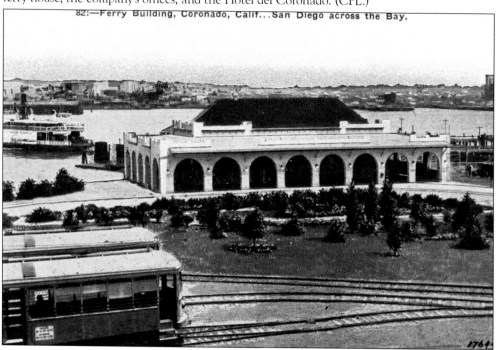

82:—Ferry Building, Coronado, Calif...San Diego across the Bay.

This ferry building, constructed in the 1920s, was referred to as the "car barn." Fashioned in a Spanish architectural style and constructed of cement and plaster, the building was the second ferry house on the peninsula and featured bench seating, restrooms, and a newsstand in a main waiting hall. The building was sold for salvage and demolished in 1949. (1906 Lodge.)

52

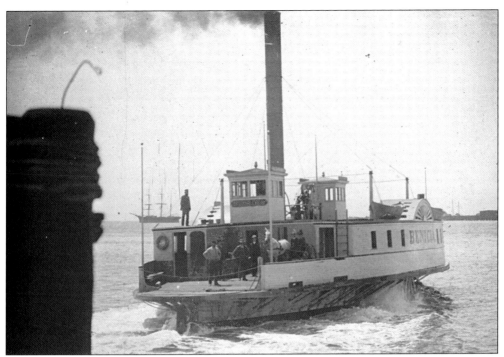

The *Benicia* served the San Diego and Coronado Ferry Company from July 1888 until July 1903 when it was replaced with a newer model. In 1893, the *Benicia* was overhauled with a new boiler and fresh paint and was put back in service until it was retired, sold, and dismantled. (CPL.)

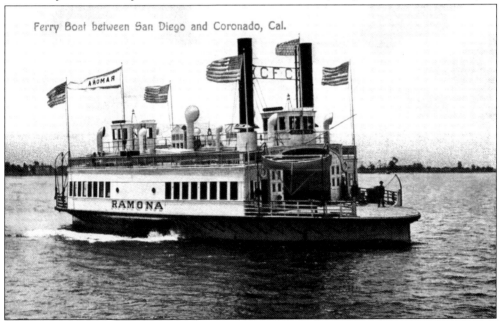

The ferryboat *Ramona* replaced the *Benicia* in 1903. The *Ramona* was the first ferry in the San Diego and Coronado Ferry Company's fleet to have incandescent lights. Once put out of commission, it was redesigned into a beer garden and café, but a few years later the *Ramona* sank at the dock under mysterious circumstances. (LHC.)

Smoking Prohibited
On Main Deck When Occupied By Automobiles

Smoking Permitted in Men's Cabin and Upper Deck Steamer Ramona, Upper Deck ONLY on Steamer Moreno

---

IN COMPLIANCE WITH THE RULES OF THE

U. S. STEAMBOAT INSPECTION SERVICE

San Diego & Coronado Ferry Company

After these signs were posted by ferry inspectors in 1919, the vice president of the San Diego and Coronado Ferry Company was reprimanded by his own crew for lighting up a cigarette on the main deck of the ferry. Allegedly owner John Spreckels was caught smoking there, too, but both men graciously abided by the rules and smoked instead in the men's cabin where it was permitted. (1906 Lodge.)

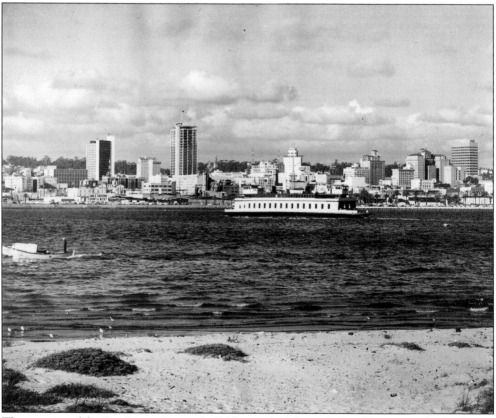

The opening of the San Diego-Coronado Bridge marked the end of an 80-year run for the ferries. The last days of Coronado's ferries were hectic because crowds of visitors wanted a final ride across the bay. Everyone, including children, realized that losing the ferries meant the end of Coronado as they knew it. (CPL.)

Four

JAPANESE TEA GARDENS

In the late 1890s, George Marsh introduced the Japanese Tea Garden to Coronado Beach. An Australian importer who owned a number of successful gardens in California, Marsh leased land from John Spreckels and brought Japanese culture to Coronado Beach. Marsh came to Spreckels with good credentials. He had been instrumental in the creation of the Japanese Village at the California Midwinter International Exposition 1894, now known as the Japanese Tea Garden in Golden Gate Park. Having lived in Japan, he spoke Japanese fluently and knew the culture well. Importing materials, artifacts, and even workmen from Japan to create the gardens, Marsh wanted to introduce Americans to the simplicity and beauty of Japan. Spreckels understood the value of offering his guests the luxuries of a tranquil garden and the opportunity to commune with nature. It was a natural tie-in with Coronado's marketing plan as a health resort, offering relaxation for the spirit.

In 1905, a series of heavy storms pummeled Coronado, badly damaging the first Japanese Tea Garden, near the Spanish Bight. Marsh negotiated with Spreckels to lease land behind the Spreckels mansion overlooking Glorietta Bay. The tea garden was bordered by the Spreckels' home on one side with Adella, Ynez, and Orange Avenues flanking the other three sides. These gardens flourished over the next 30 years, ending as the Second World War loomed and relations with Japan strained. Ira Copley, publisher of the *San Diego Union* and subsequent owner of the Spreckels mansion, bought the tea garden property from the Spreckels Company.

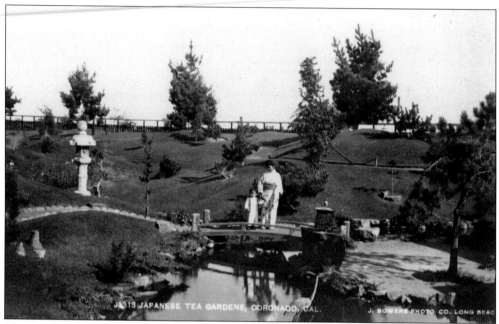

The first Japanese garden, built on a lot slightly larger than an acre, was located at the north end of Ocean Boulevard, next to the golf course near Spanish Bight. Spreckels had the Japanese garden installed next to the greens with the idea that golfers could take a break and relax with a cup of tea before going back out on the links. (CPL.)

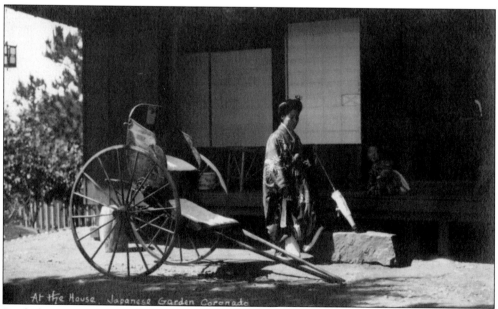

Jinrikishas, more commonly known as rickshaws, transported tourists between the Hotel del Coronado and the tea garden at the end of Ocean Boulevard. *Jinrikshas* were used in Asia for the social elite, a point that was probably not lost on Spreckels, who wanted his visitors to enjoy the classiest experience possible. (CPL.)

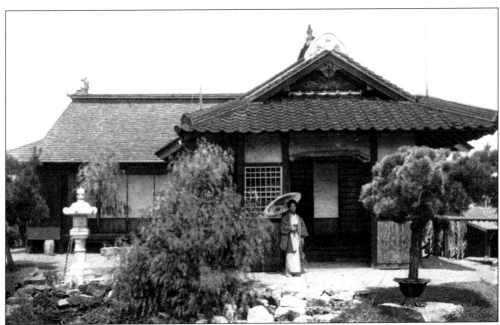

George Marsh imported nearly everything for his Japanese gardens. Wanting to intertwine the architecture of the building with the design of the gardens, March shipped in authentic summerhouses from Japan and landscaped the grounds with fishponds, lagoons, and bridges in what was meant to be a typical Far East manner. Visitors to the gardens followed Japanese tradition when entering the buildings by removing their shoes. (1906 Lodge.)

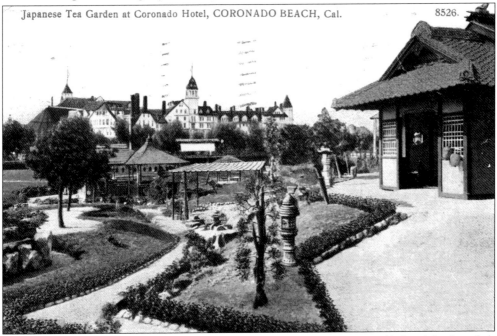

Japanese Tea Garden at Coronado Hotel, CORONADO BEACH, Cal.   8526.

After the storms in 1905 destroyed the first tea garden, a new site was created behind the Spreckels mansion. Although visitors lost the scenic ride along Ocean Boulevard, the new location was convenient as it was centrally located and allowed more room for expansion. (1906 Lodge.)

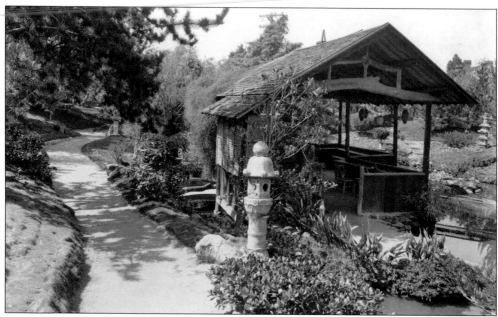

The Japanese Tea Garden was a beautiful setting in Coronado. Authentic buildings and meandering paths were landscaped with pine trees, bamboo, moss, and seasonal flowers. Stone lanterns were strategically placed, subtly symbolizing the contrasting elements of yin and yang and providing focal points in the garden. There was no electricity in the garden, so candle-lit lanterns provided illumination in the evenings, the perfect backdrop for parties and celebrations. When Japanese actor Sessue Hayakawa came to Coronado to film a movie in the famed Japanese gardens, electric lights were rigged temporarily for night shots. This technique was considered revolutionary at the time because film technology had not advanced enough to adequately capture low-light scenes, but filming at the gardens was a success and produced alluring outdoors evening scenes. (Above, CPL; below, LHC.)

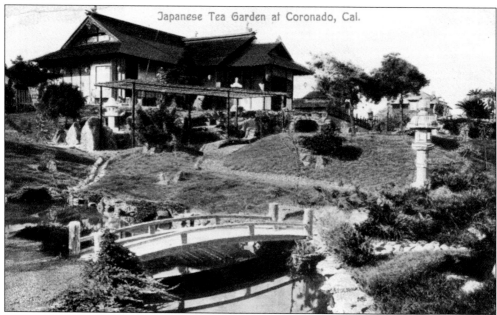

Japanese Tea Garden at Coronado, Cal.

Five

The Military
in Coronado

When Elisha Babcock and Hampton Story acquired the Coronado peninsula, the North Island was nothing more than a giant tract of flatland that had served as grazing ground for cattle in the mid-1800s. When the Hotel del Coronado was built, North Island functioned as a playground for horsemen and hunters, as well as an agriculture hub to grow food for the hotel kitchen. Potatoes grew so well there that the surplus was shipped to San Francisco.

John Spreckels owned North Island, but the federal government began utilizing it one piece at a time. It condemned some acreage during Spreckels's first years of ownership in order to build the Zuniga Jetty. By 1917, Congress passed the Condemnation Act, which permitted the federal government to take complete ownership of North Island. Spreckels fought tirelessly against the act and ultimately won a settlement of $5 million.

In 1910, prior to the Condemnation Act, aviation pioneer Glenn Curtiss received permission from the Coronado Beach Company to use North Island for three years to conduct a flying school that trained pilots. In 1911, the first naval aviator reported for duty at North Island. In 2011, North Island celebrates its 100th year as the "Birthplace of Naval Aviation." By 1935, North Island was home to four of the U.S. Navy's carriers: the USS *Langley*, USS *Lexington*, USS *Saratoga*, and USS *Ranger*.

The U.S. Army's Rockwell Field occupied one-half of North Island for about 23 years while the naval air station occupied the other half, creating, on occasion, conflict between the two military branches. In 1935, Pres. Franklin D. Roosevelt visited North Island, and ultimately it was decided that the army would relocate and the navy would claim the entire island. In the early 1940s, dredging of the San Diego Bay filled in the Spanish Bight, creating even more acreage for North Island. During that same time frame, the Naval Amphibious Base was constructed on land entirely resulted from dredging. It was the only amphibious base on the West Coast, further solidifying San Diego's role as a strategic military stronghold.

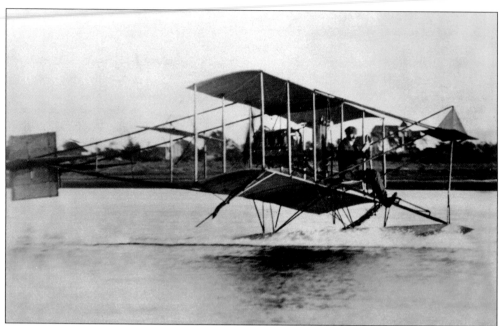

Aviator Glenn Curtiss, owner of the Curtiss Aeroplane Company in Hammondsport, New York, opened a flying school on North Island, where the first U.S. Navy pilots were trained. In this picture, taken around February 25, 1911, Curtiss successfully took off from the water and landed on the beach near the plane hangars. In this photograph is the *Triad*, a land-sea airplane with retractable wheels designed by Curtiss. (U.S. Navy.)

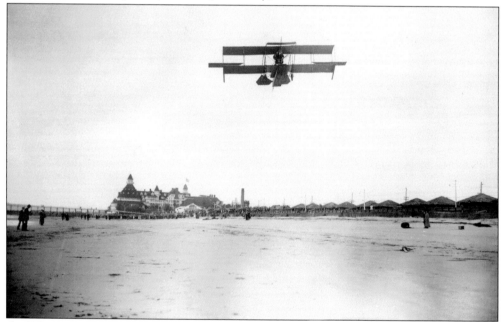

On February 26, 1911, Glenn Curtiss flew his *Triad* over the beach next to Tent City after taking off from the Spanish Bight. The day before, he successfully accomplished his first amphibian flight, taking off from water and flying around San Diego Bay twice before returning to the beach on North Island. (SDHC.)

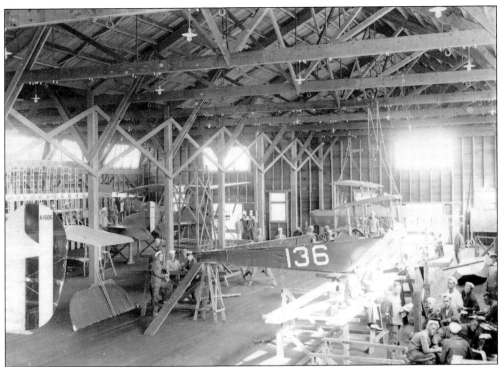

Above is an assembly and alignment hangar on North Island, as pictured in 1918. November 8, 1917, is considered the official beginning of Naval Air Station, North Island. Lt. Earl Spencer reported on this date as the first commanding officer there. Spencer was married to Wallis Spencer, better known for her later marriage to the Prince of Wales. The Spencers lived quietly on Coronado while the lieutenant worked, with very few resources, to build an air station from scratch. By the time he left his command, he had overseen the construction of multiple hangars, established a flight-training program, and completed a manual for flight instructors. Below, U.S. Navy sailors practice amphibious maneuvers on the beach in front of the Hotel del Coronado around 1918. (Both, CPL.)

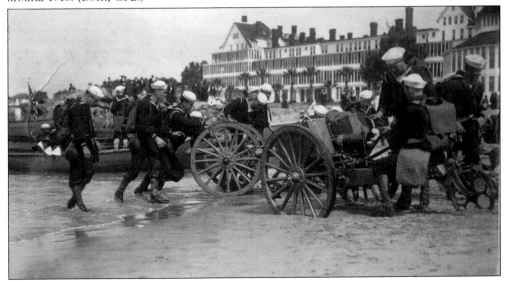

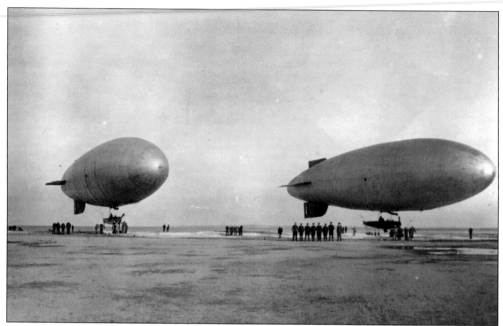

On April 20, 1915, under the guidance of Pres. Franklin D. Roosevelt, who was then Assistant Secretary of the Navy, the U.S. Navy's Bureau of Supplies and Accounts opened bids for the construction of dirigibles to be used in naval service. By 1921, North Island had three different dirigibles, dubbed "lighter-than-air aircraft," operating on the base. A large dirigible hangar was built on North Island and could be seen for miles. (CPL.)

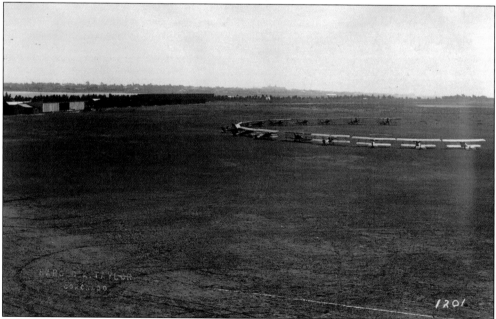

This photograph from the 1920s shows the Rockwell Field side of North Island. The navy's west beach hangars are seen to the left, and some of the army's planes form a semicircle to the right. The relationship between the army and the navy was not always cohesive on North Island, but compromises were made by both sides as military presence continued to grow there. (CPL.)

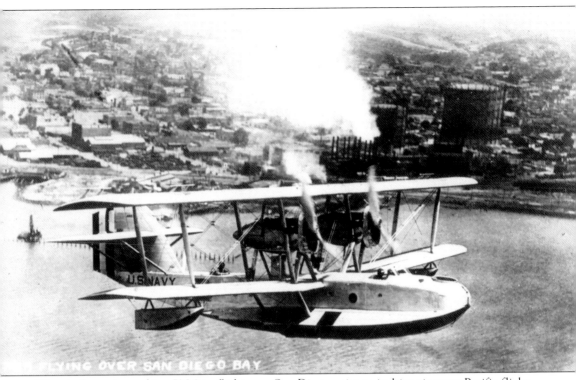

The airplane pictured is a PN-9 in flight over San Diego, prior to its historic trans-Pacific flight by Comdr. John Rodgers in 1925. Stationed at North Island, the airplane began its trans-Pacific trip in San Francisco and ran out of gas about 450 miles from Maui. Although Rodgers and his crew did not make it to the Hawaiian Islands, they had flown a total of 1,841.12 miles in the PN-9, setting a new world record. (CPL.)

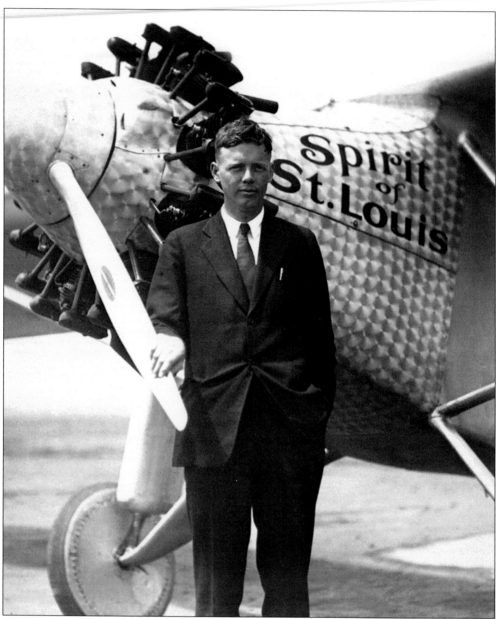

Charles Lindbergh began his historic flight to Paris by flying the first leg from North Island. His aircraft, *Spirit of St. Louis*, was built in San Diego. Because numerous other attempts to fly across the Atlantic had failed, the general public did not pay much attention as preparations were being made for the soon-to-be-historic flight. Lindbergh took off from North Island on May 10, 1927, and made his way toward the East Coast and, ultimately, Paris. After his incredible flight, he returned to San Diego in September and was regaled by thousands. A gala in his honor was held at the Hotel del Coronado, which quickly became the social event of the season. On June 11, 1927, Charles Lindbergh received the first Distinguished Flying Cross ever awarded. Since 1927, aviators honored with this medal have included former president George Bush and Sen. George McGovern, both World War II pilots, and Virgil "Gus" Grissom, a pilot during the Korean War and later a Mercury astronaut. (U.S. Navy.)

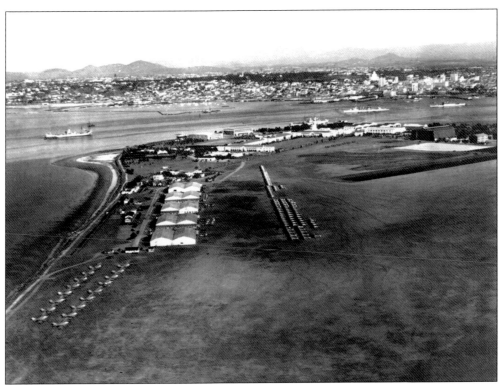

This photograph, taken in December 1928, shows the navy side of North Island: the west beach hangars with planes parked on the field (far left), the administration and barracks buildings (upper center), and the dirigible hangar and runway (upper right). In this photograph, North Island retains its original shape, but dredging of the channel would substantially fill in the area next to the west beach hangars within a few years. (U.S. Navy.)

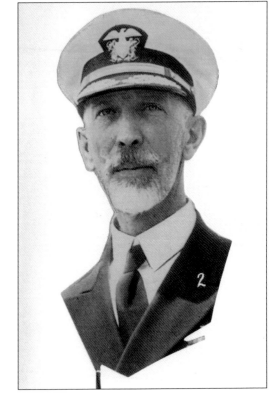

Adm. Joseph Mason "Bull" Reeves possessed great leadership and oratory skills and marketed to the general public, as well as his superiors, the importance of naval aviation. Interestingly Reeves had never been a pilot, though he did qualify as a naval aviator observer at the age of 53. (SDHC.)

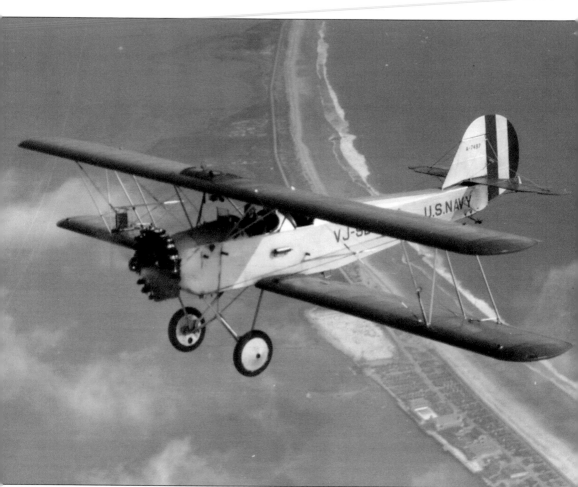

This aerial view of an NY-1 conducting aerographic flight over Silver Strand Beach was taken around 1928. Tent City is visible at bottom right. In 1928, San Diego's new municipal airport, Lindbergh Field, opened for business and brought air travel to San Diego. Civilian flyers were out in force, and stunt shows were a regular occurrence around the county. The number of women pilots was growing as well. Anne Morrow Lindbergh came to San Diego for a glider course and became the first woman in the United States to get her Class I, Class II, and Class III glider licenses—all achieved in a single flight. (CPL.)

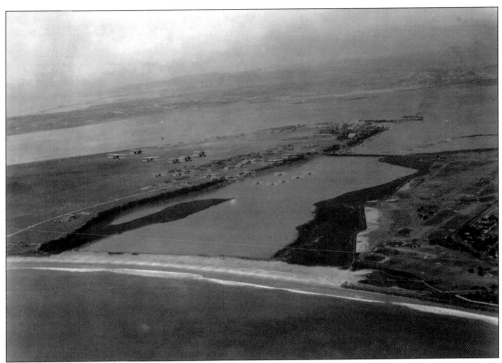

The above photograph, taken sometime around 1930, shows a military squadron flyover passing above the Spanish Bight. North Island is seen to the left, the Coronado Country Club golf course and polo field are to the right side. Naval aviation was coming to the forefront in the military's prioritization of programs. Squadrons of planes could be seen flying in formation, much to the fascination of those on the ground. The picture below shows North Island in the final years of dual occupancy by the army and the navy. As the 1930s progressed, dredge fill was added to the shoreline, broadening the perimeter of North Island. (Above, CPL; below, U.S. Navy.)

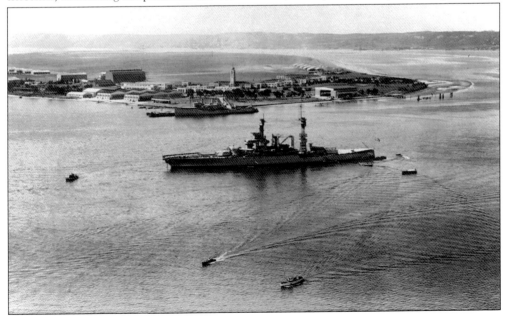

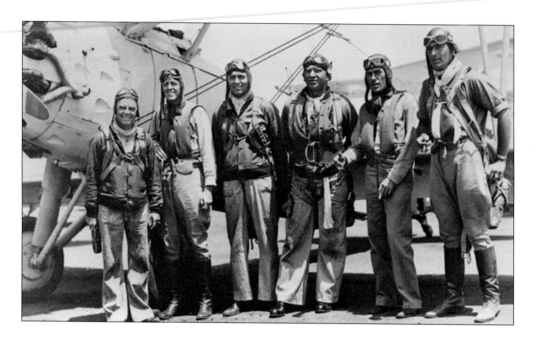

As naval aviation become more prominent to the public eye, U.S. Navy pilots were romanticized and Hollywood discovered North Island. This *c.* 1931 picture shows actors and their doubles on the set of the movie *Hell Diver*. From left to right are Cliff Edwards, Lt. John S. "Jack" Thach, Clark Gable, Wallace Beery, Lt. Herbert S. "Ducky" Duckworth, and Lt. Edward Page "Bud" Southwick. Thach would later become an admiral and was renown for the famous strategic flying maneuver he specialized in called the "Thach Weave." In the photograph below, Will Rogers, one of many celebrities who visited North Island and Coronado, went aloft in a seaplane flight over San Diego. In 1927, at a Hotel del Coronado gala, Rogers feted famed pilot Charles Lindbergh, suggesting San Diego's future municipal airport be named after him. (Both, U.S. Navy.)

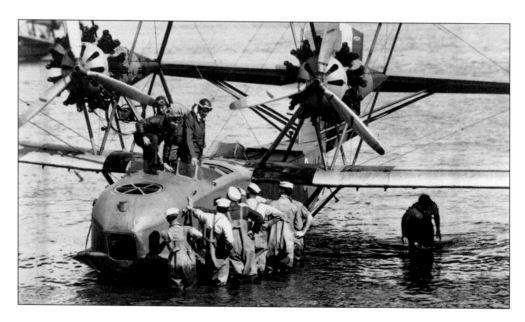

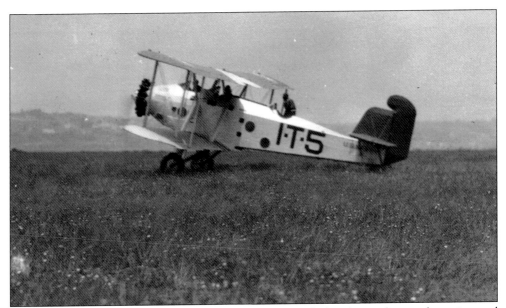

Seen on a grassy field in North Island, this Martin torpedo bomber with a single engine and three open cockpits was a large, slow craft. This airplane was in use for roughly 13 years as the U.S. Navy's main carrier strike aircraft. Only about 160 of these planes were built. Point Loma can be seen in the background. (CPL.)

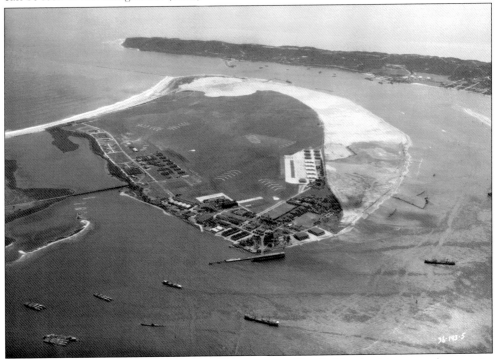

Taken around 1936, this aerial photograph illustrates North Island taking new shape as its northwesterly shore is filled by dredging of the San Diego Bay. By 1936, the U.S. Army was gone from the island and the U.S. Navy had taken over. Naval aviation was taking precedent on North Island, which was undergoing physical change as well. (SDHC.)

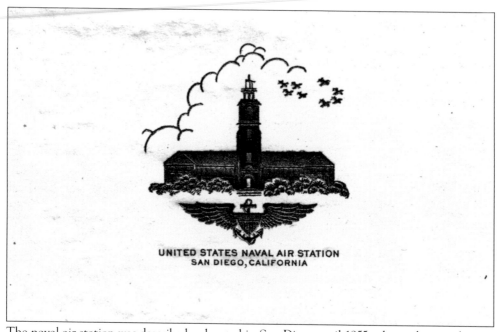

The naval air station was described as located in San Diego until 1955, when it became known as the Naval Air Station, North Island. It was granted official recognition as the "Birthplace of Naval Aviation" by a resolution of the U.S. House Armed Services Committee on August 15, 1963. (1906 Lodge.)

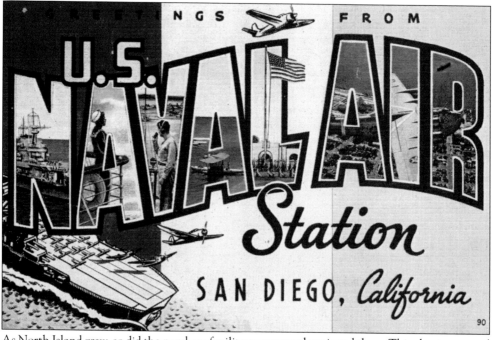

As North Island grew, so did the number of military personnel stationed there. This classic postcard provides a dutiful representation of the naval air station for sailors to send home to family members. While San Diego was a vital military city, North Island was coming into its own as an important naval hub with its strategic location and essential training programs. (1906 Lodge.)

Built in 1925, the U.S. Navy's administration building is impressive with its 110-foot-tall tower. The tower was functionally designed to carry aerological equipment and serve as the station's pre-radio control tower. The building is located in what is presently referred to as the historical district of North Island. (U.S. Navy.)

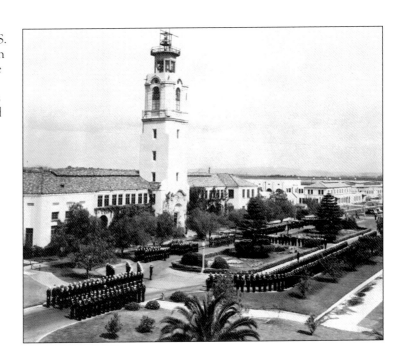

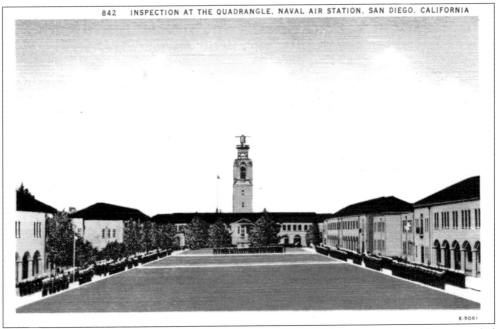

Several North Island buildings, erected during World War I, were constructed with stucco-clad walls and tile roofs, and were designed in the California Mission or Mission Revival styles. The federal government retained prominent architects Bertram Grosvenor Goodhue and Albert Kahn to design the administration building, enlisted barracks, and officers' quarters in the quad. (1906 Lodge.)

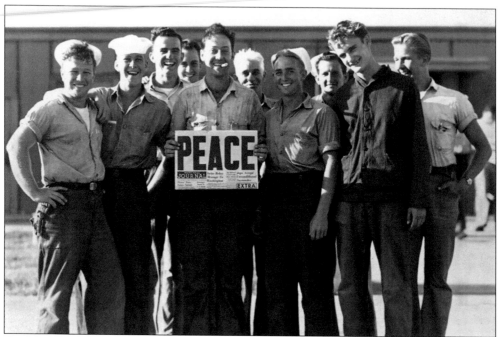

A group of sailors stationed on North Island proudly show a copy of the August 14, 1945 headlining news: the end of the war with Japan. Soon after, Coronado welcomed home its military personnel while also mourning the loss of those who did not return. North Island was a recognized cog in the military's success during World War II, further cementing its indispensable role in the U.S. Navy. (Naval Base Coronado.)

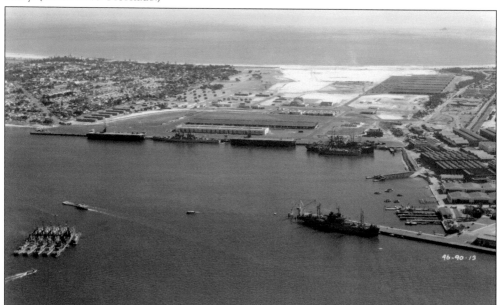

M. H. Golden Construction Company was contracted to dredge and fill in the Spanish Bight. Some of the fill was excess trash from North Island, including scrap from old aircraft. This picture, taken around 1946, shows the Spanish Bight after it was filled in. The new land area was quickly developed with administration buildings and pier-side facilities. (SDHC.)

Commissioned on January 15, 1944, the Naval Amphibious Training Base was the only amphibious base on the West Coast. Created in six months atop dredge material, the base provided a shore locale for the operations, training, and support of naval amphibious units all along the West Coast. On January 7, 1946, the base was redesignated the Naval Amphibious Base (NAB). The land was originally owned by the City of Coronado and was leased to the U.S. Navy. After some legal wrangling, the navy bought the land from the city for $850,000 in 1954. (CPL.)

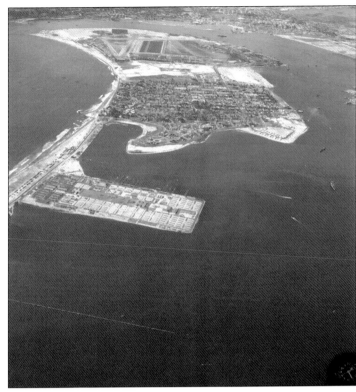

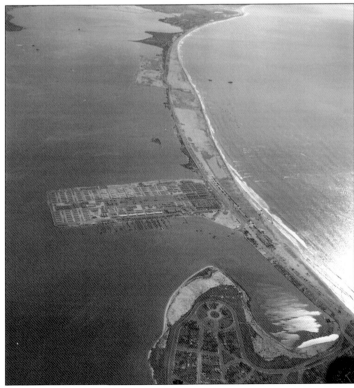

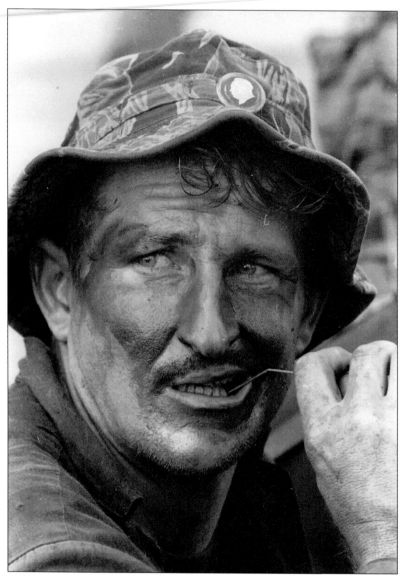

U.S. Navy SEALs in Coronado were stationed at the Naval Amphibious Base and were first housed in Quonset huts. SEAL is an acronym for sea, air, and land, representing the mission capabilities for these specialized units. Underwater Demolition Team (UDT) training, now known as BUD/S training, also occurred at NAB Coronado. Today's Naval Special Warfare operators can trace their origins to the scouts and raiders of the Naval Combat Demolition Units, Office of Strategic Services Operational Swimmers, Underwater Demolition Teams, and Motor Torpedo Boat Squadrons of World War II. SEAL Teams ONE and TWO were established on January 1, 1962, in response to Pres. John F. Kennedy's desire for military services to develop unconventional warfare capabilities. Formed entirely of personnel from UDTs, the SEALs' mission was to conduct counter-guerilla warfare and clandestine operations in maritime and riverine environments. On May 1, 1983, all UDTs were redesignated as SEAL Teams or Swimmer Delivery Vehicle Teams (SDVT). SDVTs have since become SEAL Delivery Vehicle Teams. In this photograph, a member of SEAL Team ONE takes a break during an operation on Ca Mau Peninsula, located on the southernmost tip of Vietnam, in 1968. (Chip Maury.)

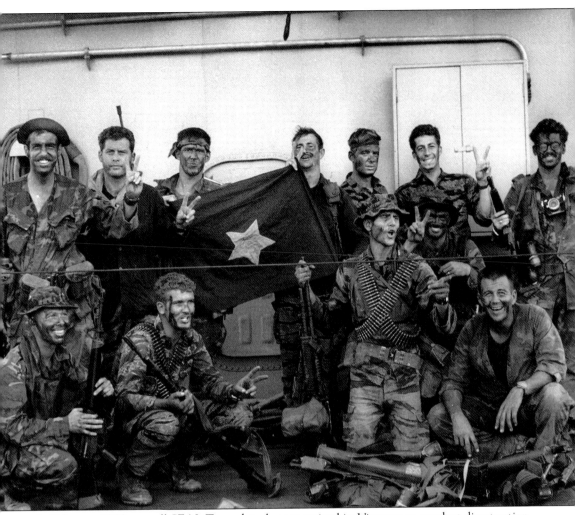

In February 1966, a small SEAL Team detachment arrived in Vietnam to conduct direct-action missions. Operating out of Nha Be, in the Rung Sat Special Zone, this detachment signaled the beginning of a SEAL presence that would eventually include eight SEAL platoons in-country on a continuing basis. Additionally, SEALs served as advisors for Provincial Reconnaissance Units and Vietnamese SEALs. In this c. 1968 photograph, SEAL Team ONE platoon members hold a captured Viet Cong flag after extracting by helicopter to a U.S. Navy Landing Ship Tank (LST) following a direct-action mission. SEALs were also involved in Apollo mission capsule recoveries and testing new technologies in underwater equipment, helping to improve equipment for military operations. (Chip Maury.)

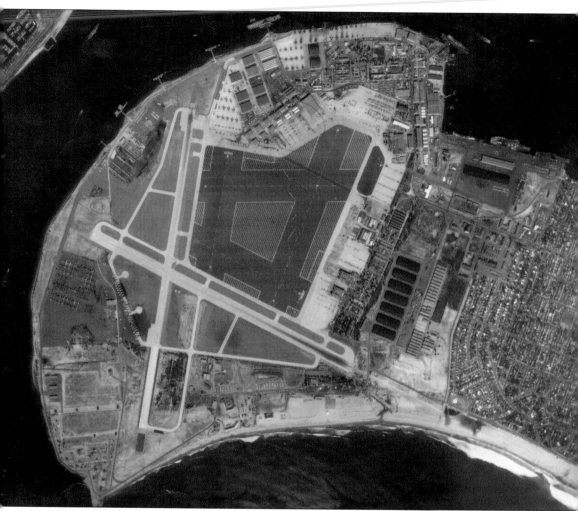

This aerial photograph, taken around 1970, shows the North Island Naval Air Station significantly altered in shape and size over the past 85 years due to dredge and fill projects. The base has developed even more with the addition of buildings and commands since the opening of the San Diego-Coronado Bridge. The administration offices, once located in the historic administration building, were moved to a new structure on McCain Boulevard, near the front gate of North Island. The giant dirigible hangar was demolished in 1971, and the flag circle located at the end of McCain Boulevard was built in 1978. The main gate is now on Third Street, and the exit is on Fourth Street. Today North Island would hardly be recognizable to someone who remembered its open fields and sparse buildings. (Naval Base Coronado.)

Six

CORONADO THROUGH THE YEARS

The transition into the 20th century marked the next phase in Coronado's evolution. In 1902, John Spreckels embarked on a massive remodel for the Hotel del Coronado, upgrading the interior and exterior with the next generation of fine furniture, carpeting, interior accessories, and landscaping.

Coronado was the destination for Hollywood stars, presidents, foreign royalty, and wealthy families. The Hotel del Coronado became a home away from home for the many families who wintered on the peninsula year after year. Tent City thrived for 40 years and became a welcomed part of the culture and community by providing activities and entertainment for guest of all ages and backgrounds.

The city of Coronado grew exponentially in the early 1900s, with regular folks moving in alongside the very wealthy residents. As the army and navy, then later just the navy, staked claim on North Island, military families moved into town and became a substantial part of the population, adding to the fabric of Coronado's demographic. World War I, the Great Depression, and World War II all took their toll on the United States, and Coronado was no exception. Loved ones who went off to fight wars were deeply missed by their families, and the wealthy faded from town as their money dried up during the Depression.

Throughout the period's tumultuous social and economic changes, Coronado held tight to its small-town allure. Children roamed freely on the island, and news always got back to their parents if they misbehaved. Neighbors knew and cared for each other. The peninsula retained a familiar and desired lifestyle that residents adored but probably took for granted, not wholly understanding the impacts of development that would inevitably rock the quiet town that they loved.

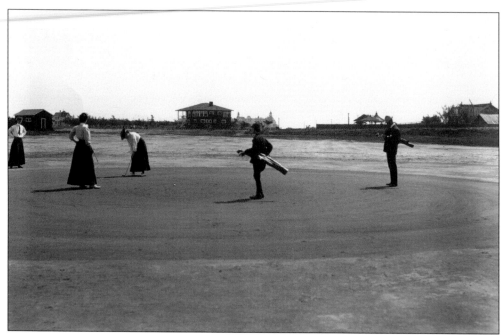

Opened in 1898, the first golf course in Coronado featured 18 holes and caddies for 50¢. Located next to the Spanish Bight at Ocean Boulevard, the golf clubhouse (back center) was a favorite destination of hotel visitors. The Japanese Tea Garden (back right) was a convenient break for a spot of tea. (SDHC.)

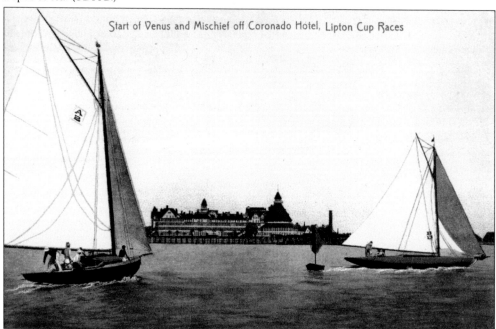

As San Diego grew, so did the sport of sailing. Started in 1904, the Lipton Cup Yacht Race was a high-profile yachting event held in the Pacific off the San Diego coast. The competition pitted the rich and famous against each other for the prestigious cup. The Coronado Yacht Club won the cup three times: in 1915, 1998, and 2001. The Coronado Cays Yacht Club won it in 1997. (LHC.)

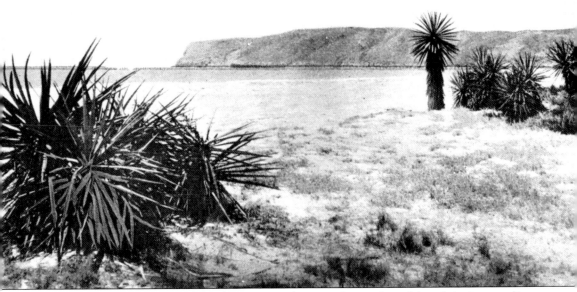

As San Diego's population and development was growing, the number of ships bringing supplies was growing too. The channel coming in to the San Diego Bay needed to be kept clear but, due to ocean currents and storms, sand kept filling the channel, requiring regular dredging. On April 15, 1893, the federal government condemned 18.05 acres on the southwestern corner of North Island to build a jetty in an effort to stop the flow of sand from the southern littoral current. A rail line was laid through Coronado so quarried rock for construction could reach the jetty. Construction started in 1894, and the jetty was built in three stages over 11 years at a cost of more than $550,000. Jutting out from the corner of North Island, the jetty extends 7,500 feet into the ocean, parallel to Point Loma. (1906 Lodge.)

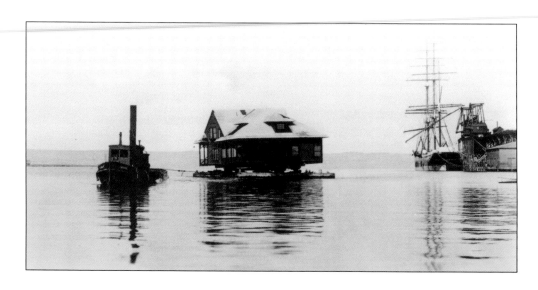

Many lots sold in Coronado belonged to people already living in San Diego. A few homes were barged across the bay to be seated on new lots. The house (above) was owned by Dr. William A. Edwards and was barged across the bay from Spreckels's coal dock to Isabella Avenue. In 1983, the Livingstone house, also known as the "Baby Del," was relocated from San Diego and placed on the lot next to the Edwards home. Houses within Coronado were moved around to different lots for various reasons. Dr. William Kneedler's house (below), at the corner of Loma Avenue and Ocean Boulevard, was moved to the corner of Tenth Street and Adella Avenue after a storm in 1905 surged water to within feet of the homes on Ocean Boulevard. (Above, SDHC; below, CPL.)

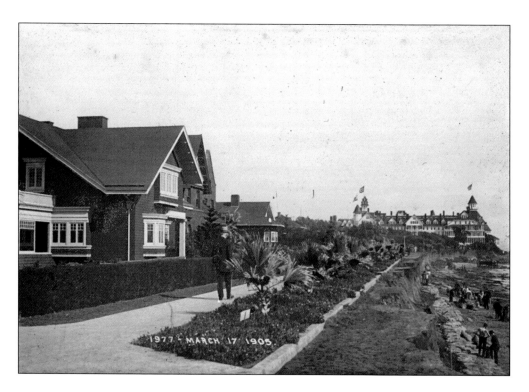

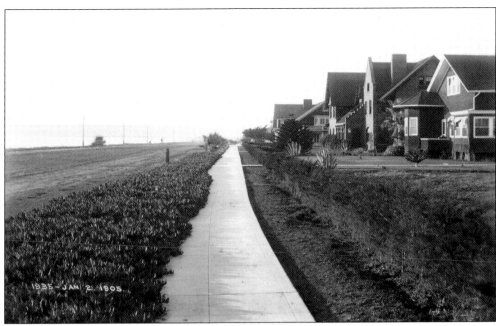

On January 4 and February 18, 1905, devastating storms hit Coronado, resulting in heavy surf eroding Ocean Boulevard. Breakers splashed against the veranda windows of the Hotel del Coronado, alarming hotel guests. Thirty thousand sandbags were placed on Ocean Boulevard and in front of the hotel but they proved useless when another strong storm hit in March, leaving extensive damage in the area. It was estimated that more than 100 feet of frontage was washed away, necessitating a solution to prevent future destruction. The picture above shows the width of Ocean Boulevard before the storms. The photograph below, taken from the perimeter of the Hotel del Coronado property, shows how much land was washed away. (Both, SDHC.)

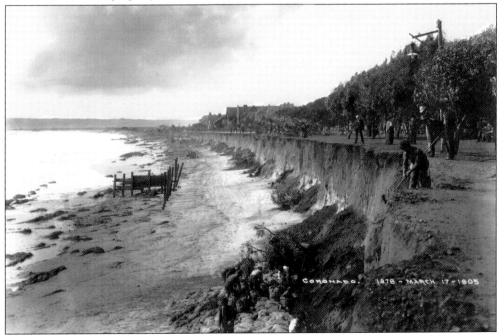

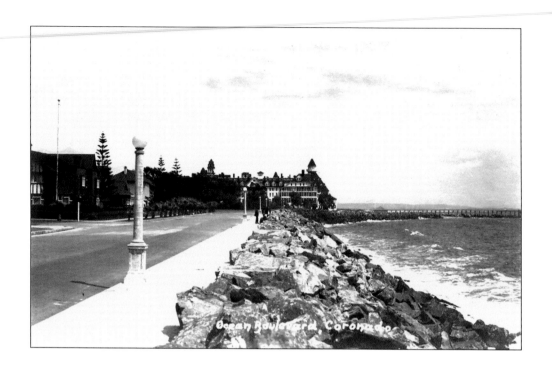

After the storms of 1905, it was decided that a seawall must be constructed. Wealthy families owned the large homes on Ocean Boulevard and were willing to pay for storm protection. The seawall was built in 1906–1907 and cost nearly $145,000. It definitely slowed the effects of erosion, but heavy seas crashing against the rock wall could sometimes still wreak havoc on Ocean Boulevard, as seen in the picture below. The two homes in the picture below still reside on Ocean Boulevard. This view was photographed looking north from near the intersection of G Avenue and Ocean Boulevard. (Above, 1906 Lodge; below, SDHC.)

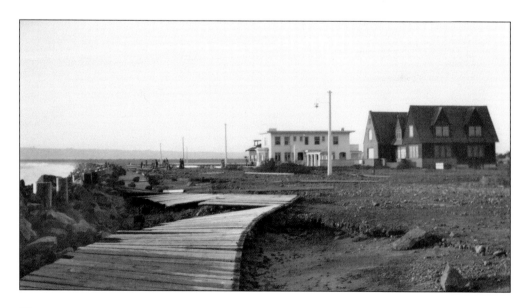

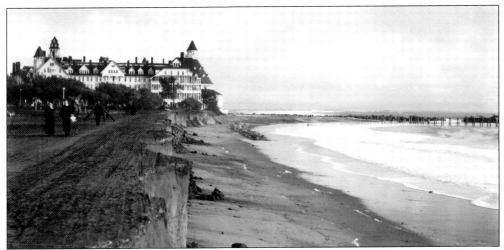

In this photograph, before the seawall was constructed, the ocean was perilously close to the Hotel del Coronado. When the rock seawall was constructed, it extended the length of Ocean Boulevard, in front of the Hotel del Coronado. When surf was particularly strong, primarily during the winter months, waves breaking against the seawall in front of the hotel led some guests to compare the booming effects of the powerful surf to the ground-shaking jolts of an earthquake. (SDHC.)

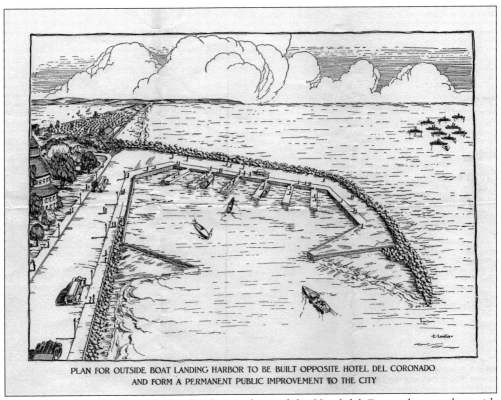

PLAN FOR OUTSIDE BOAT LANDING HARBOR TO BE BUILT OPPOSITE HOTEL DEL CORONADO AND FORM A PERMANENT PUBLIC IMPROVEMENT TO THE CITY

Plans were drafted for a small boat landing in front of the Hotel del Coronado, complete with slips and a protected harbor, but the mighty Pacific proved too dominant for the existing piers, and the harbor never proceeded beyond an enthusiastic conversation and business idea. (CPL.)

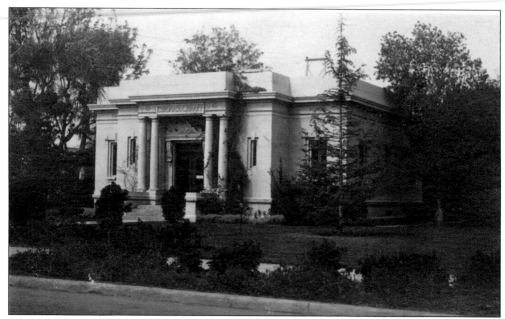

Built in 1909, the Coronado Public Library was a gift from John D. Spreckels, who also donated the block on which it sits with the condition that the city maintain the property. Designed by Harrison Albright, the library has been extensively remodeled over the years, though its original centerpiece is unaltered. (CPL.)

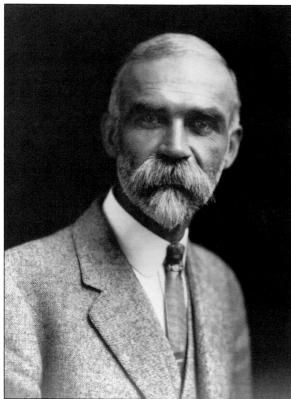

Albright was Spreckels's architect of choice because of his knowledge of reinforced concrete. Spreckels had lived through the 1906 earthquake and wanted his buildings to withstand nature's forces. Albright's distinctive style of architecture also appealed to Spreckels's because it was clean and artistic without being pretentious. Albright's designs have withstood the test of time. (SDHC.)

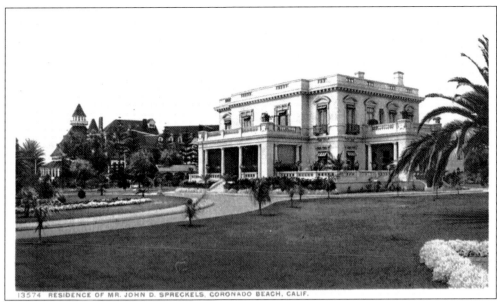

Spreckels built a mansion overlooking Glorietta Bay as his main residence when he moved to Coronado from San Francisco after the 1906 earthquake. Also designed by Harrison Albright, it exists today as the Glorietta Bay Inn. Additionally, Spreckels had Albright design a beach house on Ocean Boulevard that provides the same front row ocean views that it did 100 years ago. (LHC.)

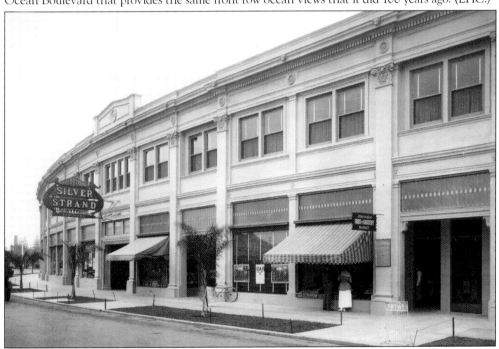

The Spreckels Building on Orange Avenue was another collaboration between Spreckels and Albright. Completed in 1917, the Beaux-Arts–style building was made with reinforced concrete. The first movie house, the Silver Strand, had a capacity of 800 people, a quarter of Coronado's population in 1920. During a restoration in 1992, Tiffany windows were found covered over with plywood. (SDHC.)

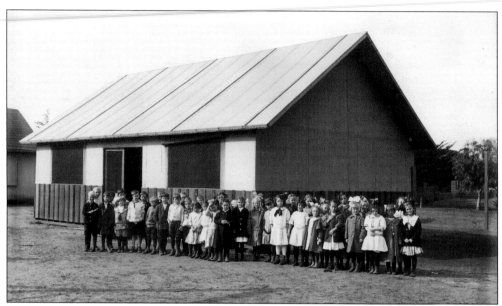

Coronado's population grew in the early 1900s causing overcrowded schools. In the picture above, a first-grade class stands in front of a temporary classroom in 1912. In June 1913, Coronado's elementary school building was completed. High school students also needed a new school, but for the time being they were moved into the old Victorian-style elementary school. Coronado High School, finally completed in 1922, was located on D Avenue on the same site where the current high school is. In 1959, the building was deemed a fire and earthquake trap, so it was demolished in 1960 to make way for new structures. The high school and middle school were combined. (Above, CPL; below, SDHC.)

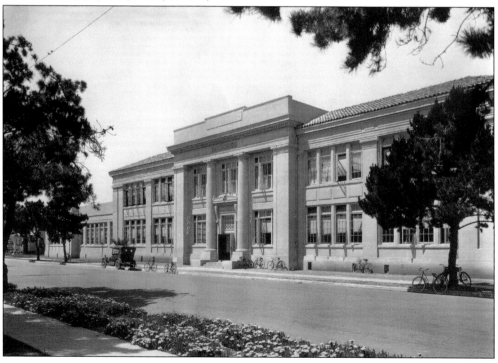

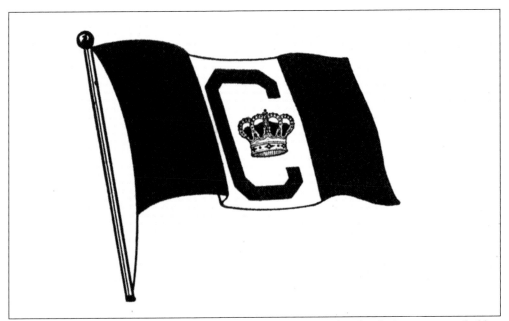

The Coronado flag was designed by Louis deRyk Millen in grade school. A contest was held to create a flag, and Millen was declared the winner. His design featured green and white colors and a gold flag. The flag has undergone minor design changes over the years, but Coronado's official flag is still proudly flown during holidays and other special events. (LHC.)

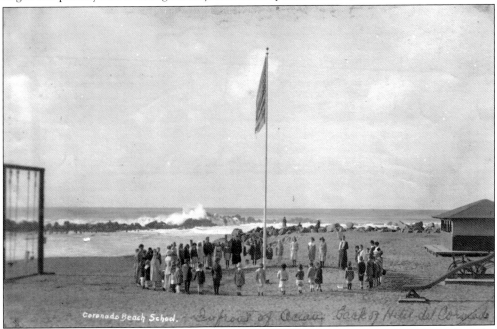

The Coronado Beach School at the Hotel del Coronado was located at the water's edge. The first private school in Coronado, it was attended by children who lived at the hotel as well as children of wealthier families on the peninsula. Students could attend the beach school up to eighth grade and, in addition to regular class work, learned French and had dance class in the hotel ballroom. (CHA.)

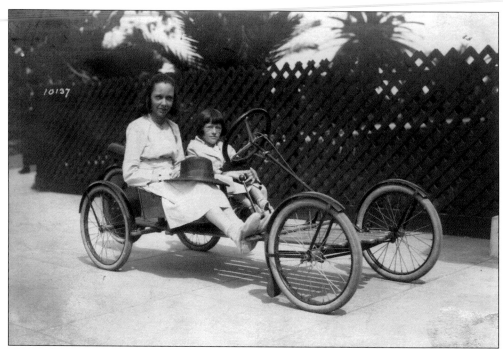

Coronado's early families left buildings, homes, and other tangible memories that live on today. In the above picture, Jane Keck Reynolds rides a go-cart-like vehicle with her best friend Barbara McClain. Reynolds family members still live in Coronado today. (CHA.)

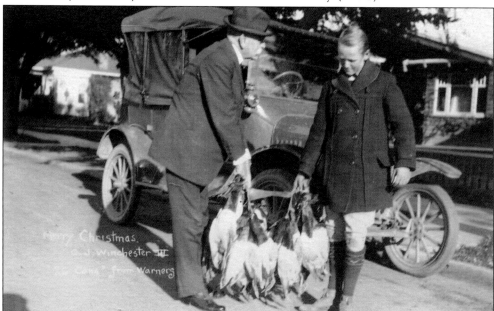

The Winchester family built numerous homes and an Italian Renaissance Revival–style building at Orange and Loma Avenues that bears the family name. Charles Winchester and his grandson Charles III are pictured standing in front of their home on C Avenue after a successful duck-hunting expedition. The home, with its distinctive rock walls, still exists on the 700 block of C Avenue. (Ky Winchester Roberts.)

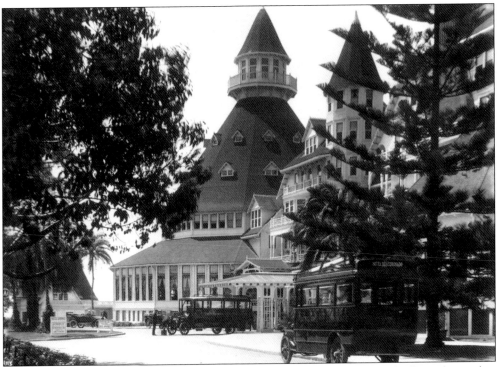

This photograph shows the Hotel del Coronado around 1914. The hotel had a fleet of vans that transported guests to various destinations. Pictured to the right side is a Norfolk pine tree—the first electrically lit outdoor tree, initially illuminated on Christmas Eve 1904, still living on the hotel grounds. (SDHC.)

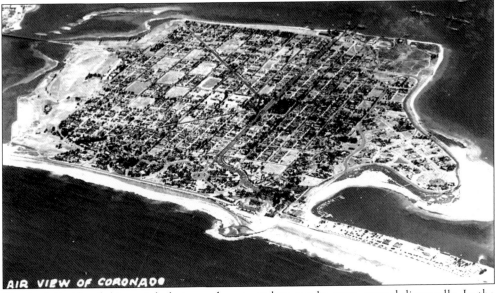

On the left side of this aerial photograph, vacant lots can be seen, spaced diagonally. In the 1940s, these blocks were developed with small homes, called Palmer Houses, which were needed to accommodate the influx of civilians and military coming to Coronado due to the wartime build-up. (1906 Lodge.)

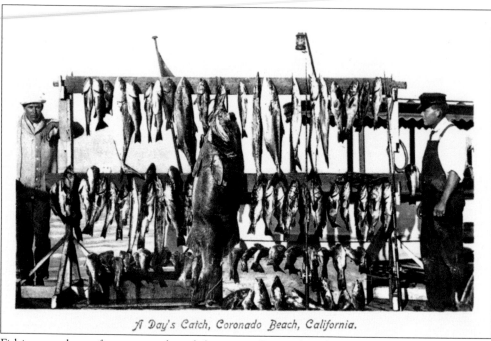

A Day's Catch, Coronado Beach, California.

Fishing was the perfect way to relax while visiting Coronado. The Hotel del Coronado arranged fishing trips for its patrons who frequently caught yellowtail, barracuda, mackerel, rock cod, and sea bass. Fishing from a long pier off the beach was a favorite pastime, but heavy winter storms eventually destroyed the pier, and it was never rebuilt. (1906 Lodge.)

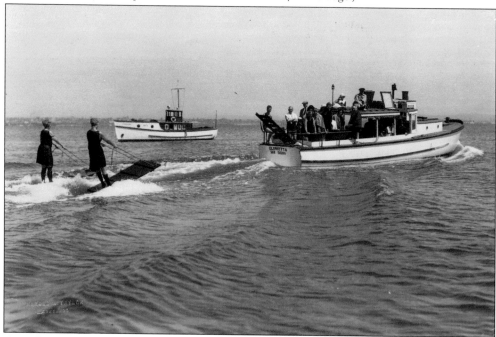

Aquaplaning was a new sport, and Coronado was the premiere setting for adventure-seekers willing to give it a try. Glorietta Bay was an ideal location for the sport since it was a protected body of water. The boathouse had a fleet of sailboats at the ready for sailors. (CPL.)

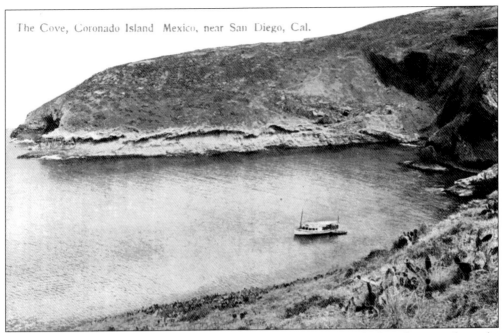

The Cove, Coronado Island Mexico, near San Diego, Cal.

The Coronado Islands were a natural wonderland that could be reached in about two hours by boat. This c. 1915 photograph depicts a typical excursion to the South Island. Visitors could explore the island to watch birds, sea lions, and elephant seals in their natural habitats. Cormorants, pelicans, and other migratory seabirds numbered in the thousands. The quarry that provided rock for Zuniga Jetty was only mined for a few years, but it became a curiosity site for hikers. Picnicking and photography excursions were popular activities, too. Sometimes a glass-bottomed boat was towed behind the excursion vessel to offer visitors a glimpse of the sea life below the ocean's surface. (Above, LHC; below, 1906 Lodge.)

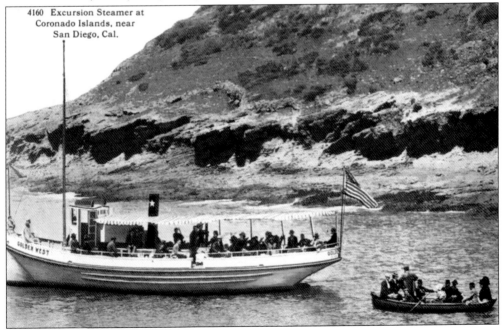

4160 Excursion Steamer at Coronado Islands, near San Diego, Cal.

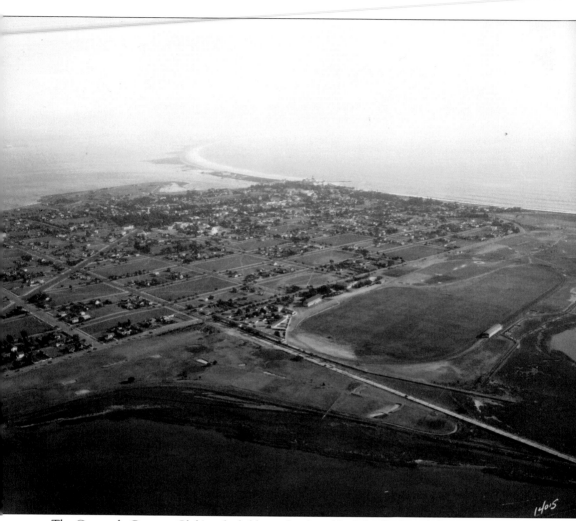

The Coronado Country Club's polo field was developed by John D. Spreckels in the early 1900s. The polo field extended from Fourth Street to Eighth Street, west of Alameda Boulevard. This picture, taken in 1920, shows the causeway to North Island connected from Fourth Street, later becoming the main road into North Island, called McCain Boulevard. The bottom of the picture shows the water's edge at the Spanish Bight and the golf course, which was moved to this location after the 1905 storm. The Coronado Country Club remained a centerpiece of social life for many years, hosting polo matches, horse shows, rodeos, golf tournaments, and other social gatherings. Millionaires and celebrities congregated here while the small town folks ogled at the extravagance. By January 1950, times had changed significantly. Plans were presented by developers to build residential housing where the Coronado Country Club once stood. By March of that year, all of these landmarks that had played significant roles in Coronado's history were demolished. (CPL.)

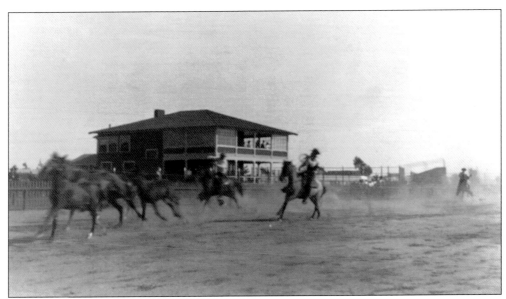

The polo fields hosted a variety of events involving horsemen. One event, called Gymkhana, featured trick riding, races, and riding exhibitions. Riding entries from all over California came to compete, raising money to fund war veteran programs and other service organizations. (CPL.)

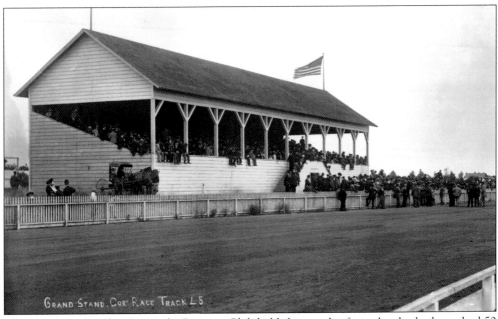

The grandstand at the Coronado Country Club held thousands of people who had watched 50 years of events that included the historic flights of Glenn Curtiss, the Coronado National Horse Show, and two renowned polo events: the Pacific Coast-All American Trophy and California Challenge Trophy.

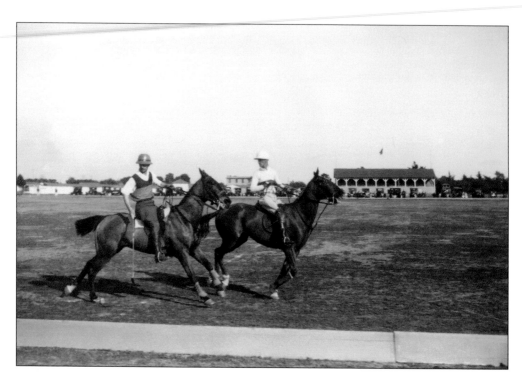

Walter Dupee, who lived in the Richards/Dupee mansion at 1015 Ocean Boulevard, was instrumental in kindling the polo scene in Coronado. In the picture below, polo players, including Charlie Chaplin (far right), pose with their horses. Chaplin lived a quiet life in Coronado at his house that still stands at the corner of Tenth Street and Olive Avenue. (Above, SDHC; below, CPL.)

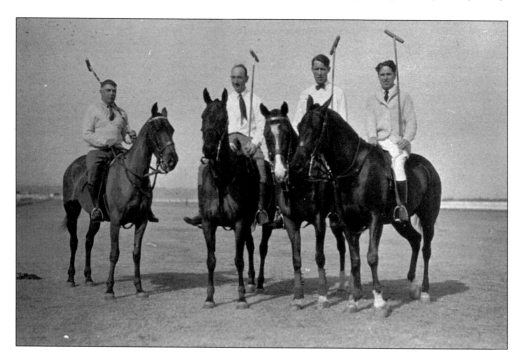

The Coronado National Horse Show was a chic attraction that catered to the high society of San Diego. The five-day show featured polo ponies, stock horses, a breeding division, hunters and jumpers, and harness ponies. The show also spotlighted special entertainment such as movie stars and trick horse riders. Owners and competitors brought their horses from as far as New Mexico, Texas, and Missouri. The net proceeds of the show were donated to charity. Box holders were the movers and shakers of San Diego, including the Scripps, Fitch, Wegeforth, Fleet, and Jessop families. (At right, 1906 Lodge; below, CPL.)

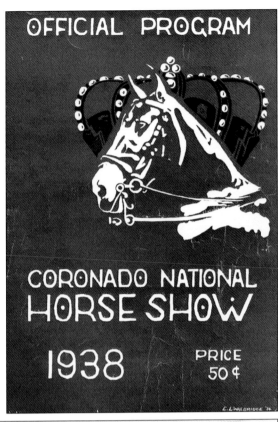

OFFICIAL PROGRAM

CORONADO NATIONAL
HORSE SHOW
1938   PRICE
              50 ¢

E. L. WALBRIDGE

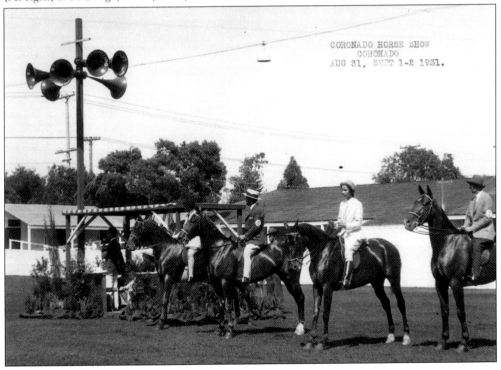

CORONADO HORSE SHOW
CORONADO
AUG 31, SEPT 1-2 1931.

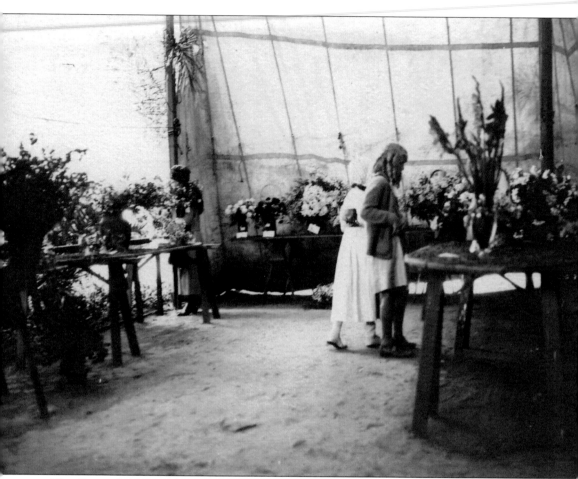

The Coronado Flower Show, a tradition dating back to 1922, was started by local photographer Harold Taylor at the request of his wife. He formed the Coronado Floral Association, borrowed canvas tents from North Island, and set them up in the East Plaza, now known as Spreckels Park. People speculated there would not be enough flowers to put on a flower show but the event touted plenty of entries, and it quickly became a rousing success. Later the City of Coronado purchased tents that were used for the show, but over time the repair and labor costs of erecting the tents year after year became too costly. (CHA.)

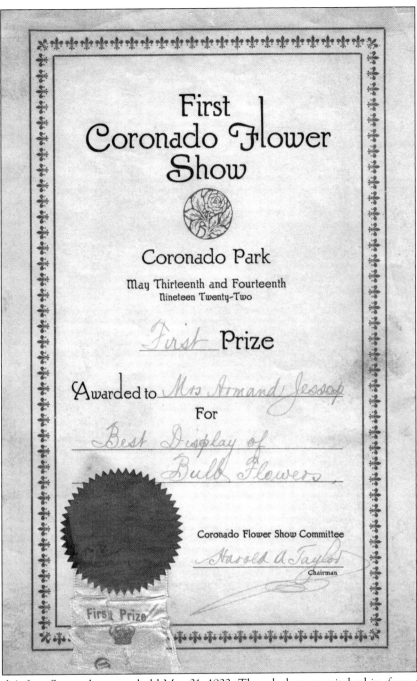

First Coronado Flower Show

Coronado Park

May Thirteenth and Fourteenth
Nineteen Twenty-Two

First **Prize**

Awarded to *Mrs Armand Jessop*

For

Best Display of Bulb Flowers

Coronado Flower Show Committee

Harold A Taylor
Chairman

First Prize

Coronado's first flower show was held May 31, 1922. The whole town pitched in, from the Boy Scouts who guarded the show to the Hotel del Coronado, which donated tables and trellises. A flower show parade was held for a few years in the 1930s. Initially there was no entry fee for the show, but as it expanded so did the costs of organizing it, so eventually showgoers handed over 10¢ per person to wander among the dozens of tents of flowers. This first-place certificate is from the peninsula's first Coronado Flower Show in 1922. It was won by Elsie Jessop and is signed by flower show chairman Harold Taylor. (CHA.)

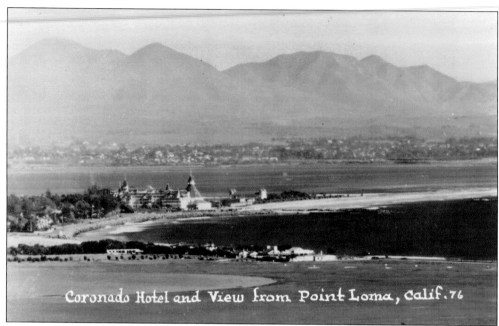

Coronado Hotel and View from Point Loma, Calif. 76

This photograph, taken from Point Loma, shows North Island and Coronado during the 1930s. The stand of eucalyptus trees—many of which still grow today—on the bluff overlooking Spanish Bight was planted at the end of the 19th century by the Hotel del Coronado to hide the flatlands of North Island. The Hotel del Coronado and Tent City are seen off in the distance. (LHC.)

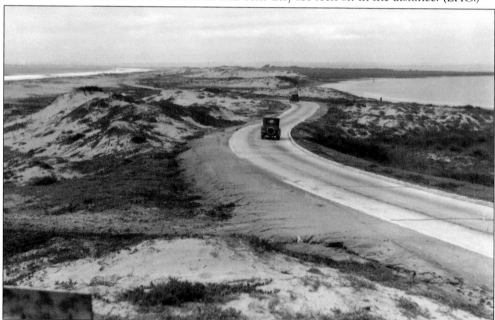

This picture of the Silver Strand was taken in the late 1920s. Looking north, it shows the area just south of the present-day Coronado Cays, formerly known as the Rancho Carrillo tidelands. Before development of the cays, the site had formerly been a dump and a hog ranch. The State of California created a state park on the Silver Strand in 1931 after the Spreckels Company presented land to the California State Parks Commission. (SDHC.)

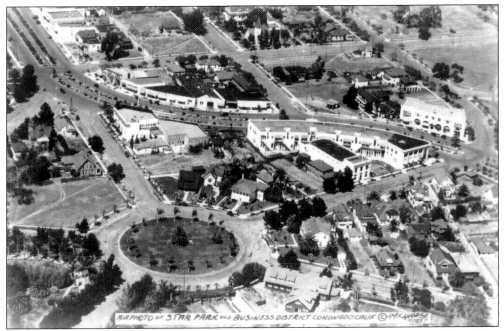

With its five access roads, the center of Star Park resembles a star, hence its name. When Star Park Circle was originally planted, hedges in the park were trimmed in the shape of a star with a large fountain in the middle. Many of Coronado's oldest historic homes still remain on Star Park and its nearby streets. (CPL.)

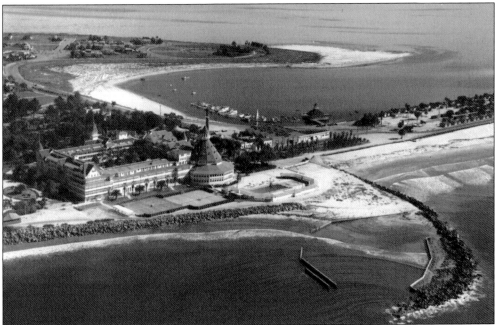

This aerial photograph from 1936 shows the tennis courts and saltwater pool at the Hotel del Coronado's Beach and Tennis Club, built on the beach in 1934. Their construction coincided with the demolition of the old saltwater plunge from the hotel's earliest days. Tent City (far right) would close at the end of the decade. (CPL.)

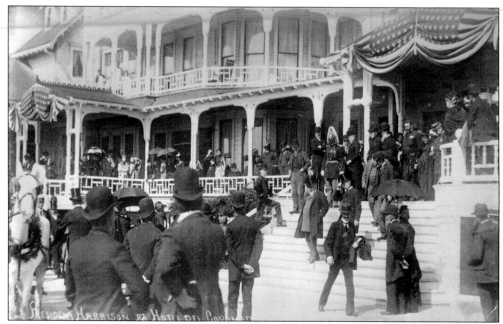

In 1891, Pres. Benjamin Harrison became the first American president to visit the Hotel del Coronado. He is pictured coming down the entrance stairs to the hotel. Eleven U.S. presidents have visited the Hotel del Coronado. Richard Nixon hosted the first state dinner away from the White House at the hotel in 1970. Ronald Reagan held a summit there in 1982. (CPL.)

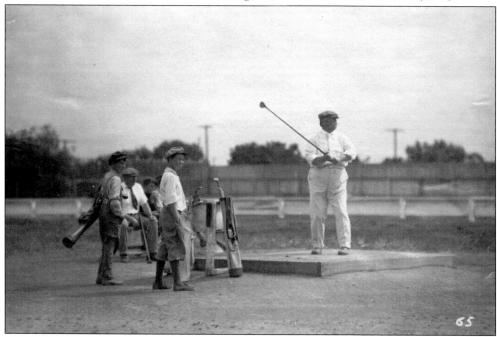

Pictured is Pres. Howard H. Taft (1909–1913) playing golf at the Coronado Country Club, caddies at the ready. In 1900, Taft had a sister living in Coronado whom he visited. He returned to the peninsula in 1915 to stay at the Hotel del Coronado, presumably to attend the Panama-California Exposition in Balboa Park. (CHA.)

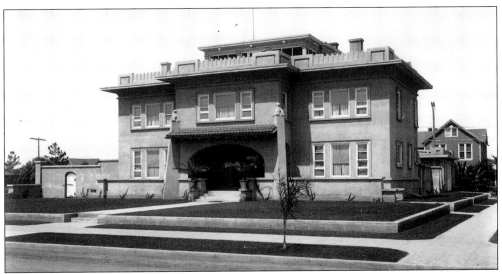

Architect Harrison Albright designed this Italian Renaissance Revival home in 1907 for John Spreckels's attorney, Harry Lewis Titus. Located at the west corner of Orange Avenue and Eighth Street, the home also had a roof garden complete with sleeping accommodations. The house visible in the background (far right) is still standing at Eighth Street and D Avenue. (CHA.)

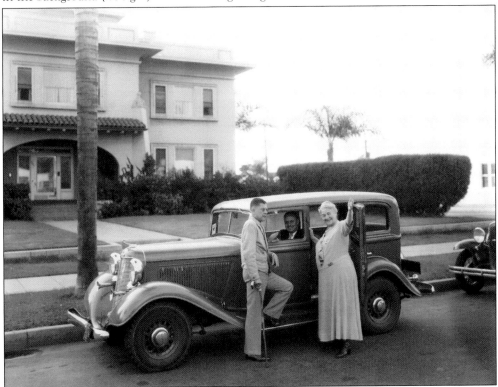

Titus sold the home to Madame Ernestine Schumann Heink, world-famous opera singer and beloved personality. She lost two sons in World War I, one fighting on the American side, the other fighting for the German army. During World War II, she became known as "Mother" because she was a tireless supporter of the troops. The home was razed in 1936 after her death. (SDHC.)

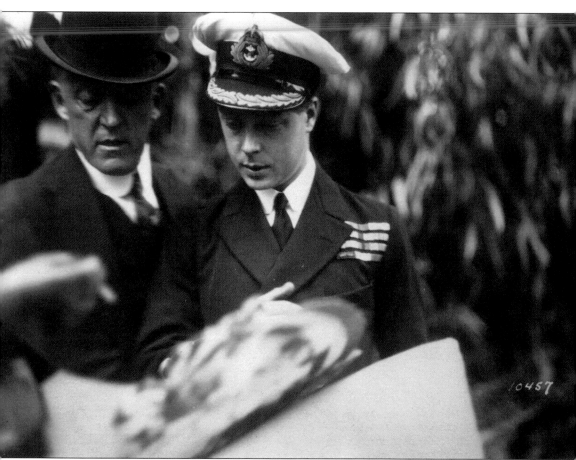

Edward, Prince of Wales, visited Coronado on April 7, 1920, on his way to Australia. San Diego proved to be a perfect port to refuel and supply his ship, *Renown*. Though his visit was called "unofficial," it was highly anticipated by the residents of San Diego. When he disembarked that afternoon, it was his first time on the West Coast. A ritzy dinner was held in his honor at the Hotel del Coronado. Although his future wife, Wallis Warfield Spencer Simpson, had lived in Coronado a few years prior (her husband was the first commanding officer of North Island), the two did not meet during his short visit. In 1974, Charles, Prince of Wales, visited Coronado to try his hand at surfing. In 1983, Queen Elizabeth and Prince Philip arrived in San Diego aboard the USS *Brittania*, one of many stops on their tour of the West Coast. (CPL.)

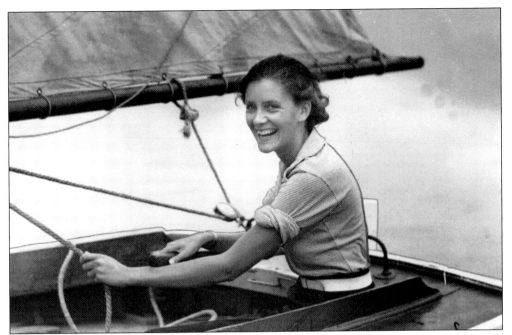

With great weather year-round, Coronado youth were an active bunch. Boating was a top-notch activity with the local yacht club, boathouse, and Tent City contributing to other activities on the water. Coronado High School sports began to take form as well, with baseball and football team rosters growing lengthier each year. (CHA.)

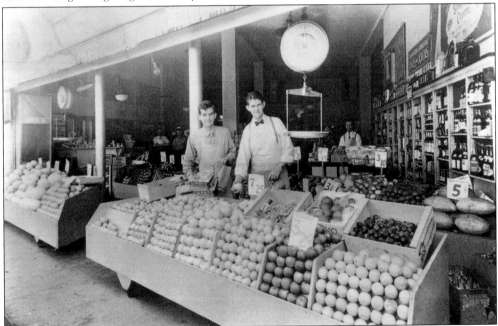

Pete's Market was located at 170 Orange Avenue and sold fresh fruits and vegetables, offering "Nothing But the Best," as advertised in the *Coronado Citizen* newspaper, to its clientele. Small shops such as Pete's were locally owned and customer oriented. It was typical for shopkeepers to know their customers by name. (SDHC.)

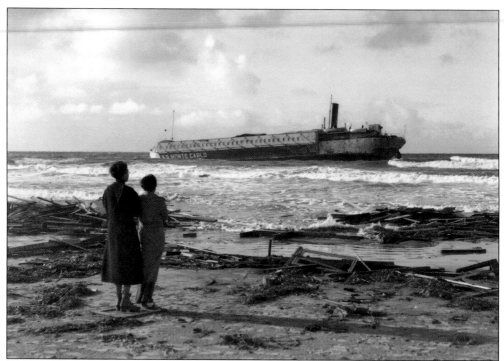

In 1936, gambling was a provocative issue in San Diego. The 300-foot-long, concrete-hulled *Monte Carlo* was one of three casino ships anchored in international waters, 3 miles from shore, off Point Loma. Partakers were transported to the ship on water taxis. On New Year's Eve 1936, a severe storm hit the area and by New Year's Day 1937, the *Monte Carlo* had run aground near the south end of Tent City. Today the deteriorating hull of the *Monte Carlo* is exposed at low tide during certain times of the year. (Above, SDHC; below, LHC.)

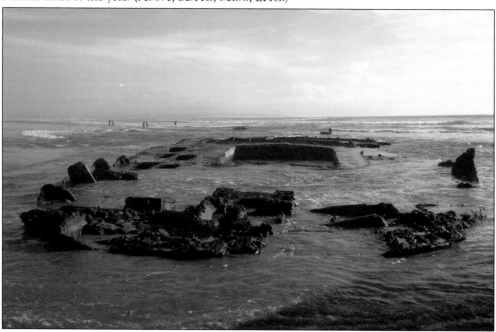

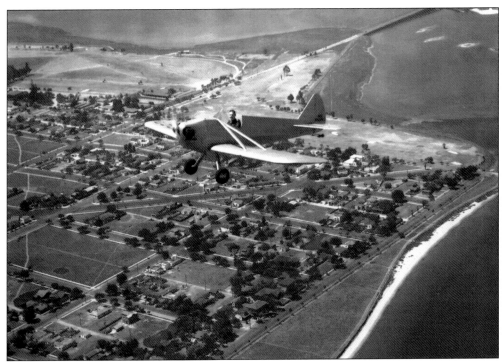

This c. 1938 photograph depicts Coronado a few years before the military began appropriating land on North Island. Visible landmarks are the North Island causeway, which was built as a railroad trestle in 1887 and became a road in June 1918; the Coronado Country Club golf course; the San Diego Bay shoreline before any homes had been built; and Palm Avenue running diagonally across. (SDHC.)

The Coronado stables were located at Alameda Avenue and Fourth Street near the Coronado Country Club. Suzie Heap used to ride horses all the way around Coronado, stopping by her house on First Street. In this picture, she is on Coronado Beach with her horse Honey. She and her friends participated in the children's horse show, entertaining spectators by square-dancing on horseback. (Suzanne Heap.)

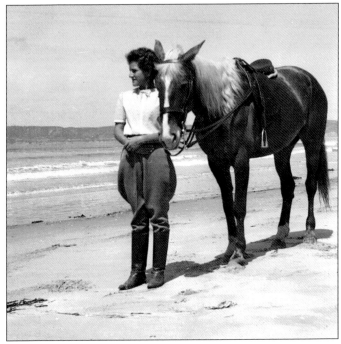

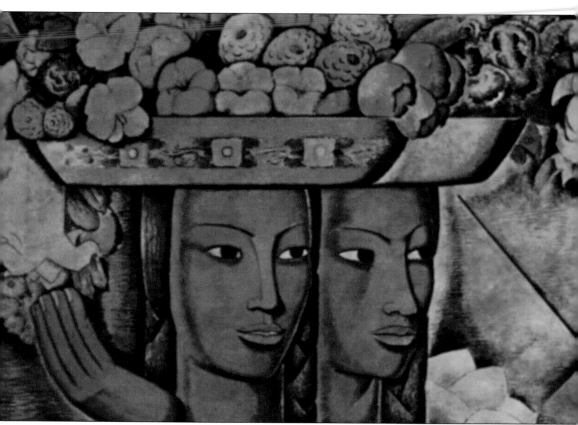

Mexican painter Alfredo Ramos Martinez painted this mural, titled *Flores de Mexico*, for the La Avenida restaurant in Coronado. In 1938, Martinez was commissioned by Albert Bram to paint more murals for the restaurant. One mural was lost during a remodel, but the remaining were still intact at the restaurant when new owners, in 1992, sought to preserve the pieces of art

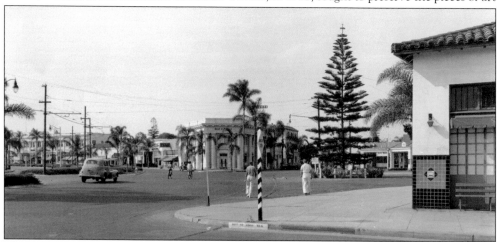

This photograph shows Orange Avenue from Tenth Street in the 1940s. Coronado's downtown appearance from then until present day boasts more similarities than differences. Today the Coronado Historical Association is headquartered in the center building. The city's beloved Christmas tree is pictured slightly to the right. (SDHC.)

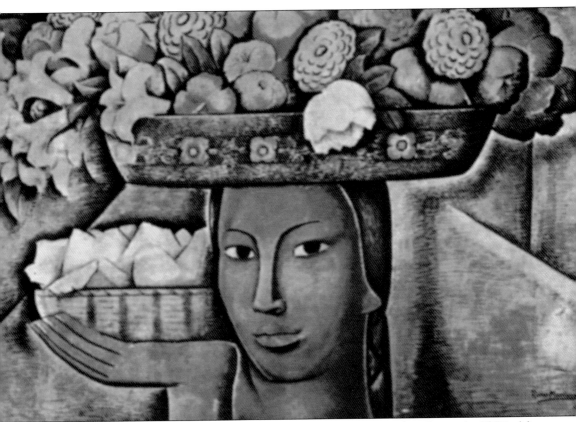

before they redecorated the interior. Images were restored and returned to Coronado. *El Dia del Mercado* and *La Canasta de Flores* were installed in the Coronado Public Library as part of the library renovation and expansion project. (John Munns Photography.)

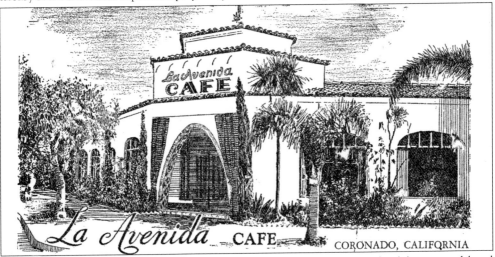

La Avenida restaurant was a longtime, popular restaurant that served celebrities and local families. The Martinez murals were focal points in the restaurant. The "Jack salad," a version of the Caesar salad made famous at Caesar's Restaurant in Tijuana, was a signature dish at La Avenida. (LHC.)

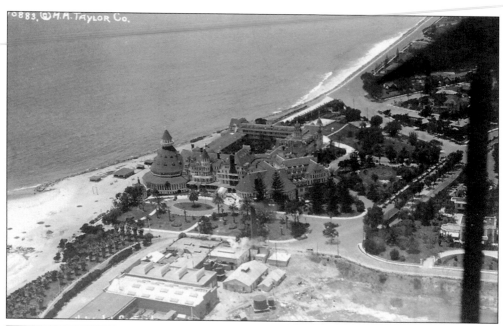

This aerial view of the Hotel del Coronado shows the configuration of Orange Avenue before it was rerouted to go straight down the hill by Glorietta Bay and connect to the Strand Highway. (CPL.)

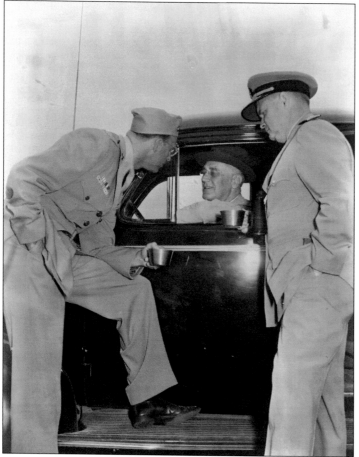

Pres. Franklin D. Roosevelt visited Coronado a number of times for official business and also to visit his son who was stationed there. When he arrived and departed Coronado, it was by way of ferry, with sailboats following alongside. (CPL.)

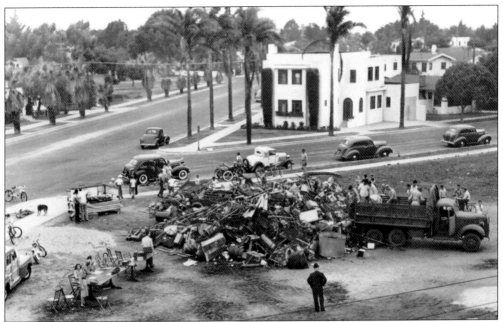

In 1942, the War Salvage Committee of Coronado collected more than 20 tons of metal, rubber, grease, and newspapers piled at the corner of Sixth, Palm, and D Avenues, which were to be converted into war supplies. Coronado was a navy town with a strong sense of duty and community because so many of its husbands and fathers were in the military. (SDHC.)

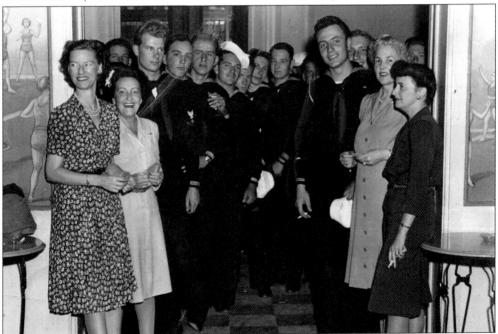

During World War II, the Hotel del Coronado hosted weekly gatherings for military men. Local women entertained their male-dominated audiences with dancing, dining, and socializing; sometimes romances and marriages resulted. Because rationing was in place, all lights were ordered to be turned off after dark. (CHA.)

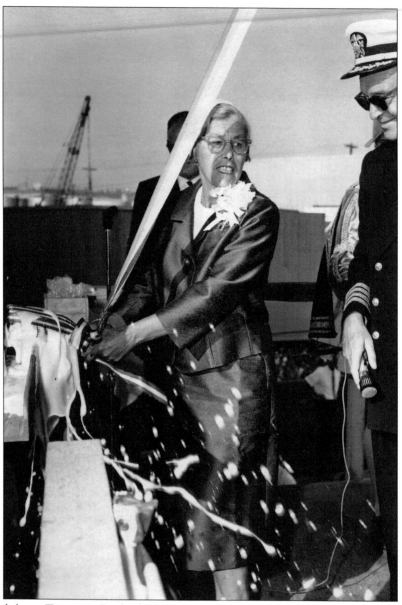

The Amphibious Transport Dock, the USS *Coronado* (LPD-11), was launched on July 30, 1966. Built at Lockheed Shipbuilding Company in Seattle, Washington, the USS *Coronado*'s sponsor was Eleanor Reynolds Ring, widow of Adm. Stanhope Cotton Ring. The ship was named to honor the patriotic people of Coronado. Eleanor Ring was the daughter of U.S. Navy pay director Ziba Wells Reynolds and Ruth Isabelle "Belle" Stewart, who led the grand march at the opening of the Hotel del Coronado. Her grandfather, among other notable achievements, was a partner in the building of the first shipyard in San Diego, located at the northeasterly point of North Island, next to the Spanish Bight. The family's naval tradition continued on with her two sons. She was a councilwoman for the City of Coronado, as well as an active member in community and political organizations. A third Coronado namesake ship, the USS *Coronado* (LCS), a littoral combat ship, will be commissioned in 2013. The sponsor of this new ship is her daughter, Susan Ring Keith. (Susan Ring Keith.)

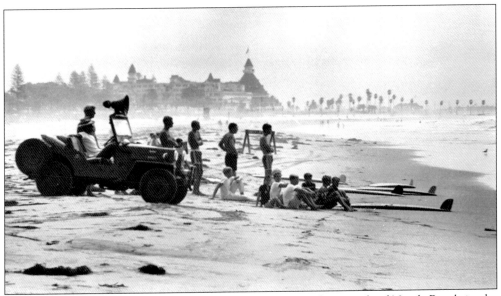

Surfing is a dominant aspect of life in Coronado. In this photograph of North Beach in the mid-1960s, participants watch a surfing contest. Some of the surfers pictured still live and surf in Coronado today. The Hotel del Coronado is featured prominently in the background with its property line of palm trees on the beach, before Coronado Shores condominiums were built. (John Elwell Collection.)

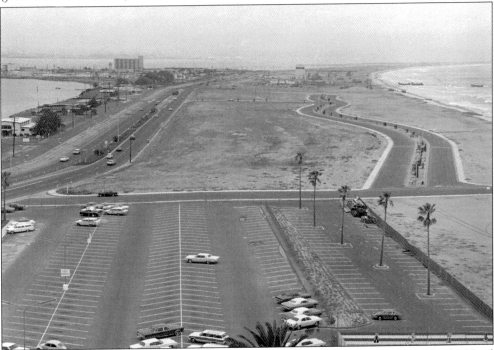

Where Tent City once stood, the Coronado Shores condominiums now rest. In 1964, the Hotel del Coronado Company received approval to build high-rise apartments on the beach just south of the hotel. Construction began in 1970, the year after the San Diego-Coronado Bridge was built. (CPL.)

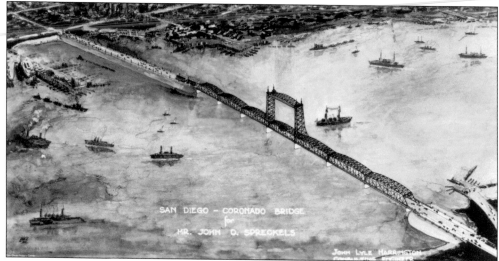

From Coronado's earliest years, the issue of transportation to and from Coronado has been addressed frequently. The Spreckels Company commissioned a drawing of a proposed drawbridge from Market Street in San Diego to First Street and Alameda Boulevard in Coronado, but the navy did not agree with the proposal. In 1958, the idea of a bay crossing in the form of a tunnel or bridge was protested by residents of Coronado. While some people argued that a crossing was needed for the economic well-being of the community, residents knew that a highway tunnel or bridge would bring dramatic change to the peninsula since it would become so easily accessible. After eight more years of controversy between the State of California, the U.S. Navy, and the residents of Coronado, construction of a new bridge began. (Both, SDHC.)

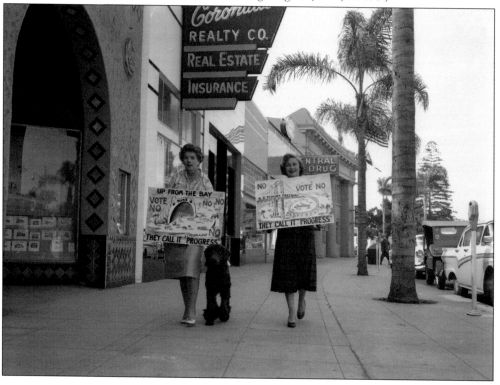

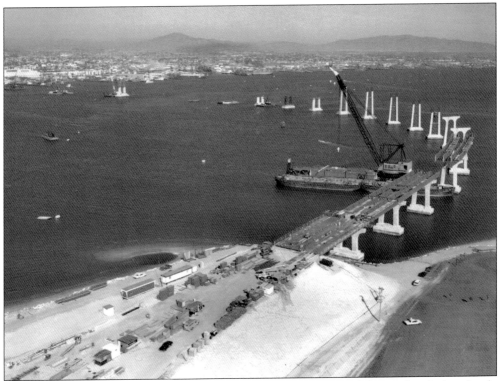

In 1966, construction was underway for a new bridge. Residents uneasily listened to the ker-chunk, ker-chunk, ker-chunk of concrete pilings being driven into the bay's sandy bottom. Measuring 2.12 miles long with a 90-degree arc, the bridge cost $48 million to build. The sheer size of the project seemed beyond description to peninsula residents, who realized their small-town beach community was at the end of an era. (SDHC.)

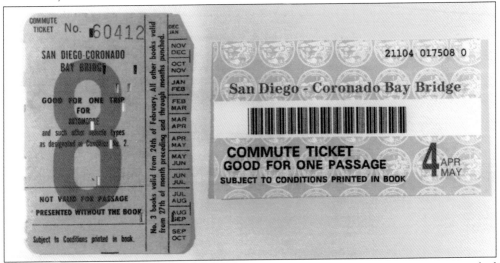

The San Diego-Coronado Bay Bridge, as it was officially known, opened on August 3, 1969; it marked the end of ferry service to and from the peninsula. Drivers paid cash to cross the bridge each way, but Coronado residents and regular commuters had the option of buying a book of tickets at a reduced price. Once the bridge bonds were paid off, the tolls were removed eventually. (CHA.)

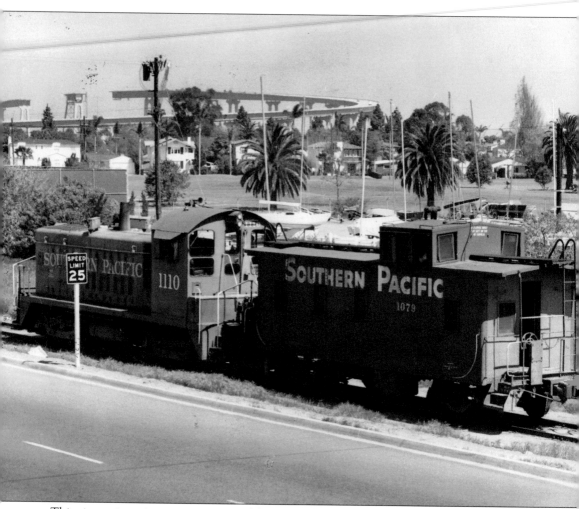

This picture is a prime representation of the past and future converging in Coronado. Trains were the traditional mode of transportation on the peninsula, though looming in the background is the state-of-the-art San Diego-Coronado Bay Bridge being pieced together. The first train on Coronado ran from the ferry landing to the Hotel del Coronado, introducing people to Coronado as they rolled across town. Freight was distributed throughout Coronado by train, and rocks were hauled from Sweetwater Quarry for the Zuniga Jetty and other seawall projects. North Island, and later the Naval Amphibious Base, were supplied by regular train deliveries. Trains were a key part of Coronado's history until 1970 when the ceremonial spike was pulled out of the tracks, marking the end of train travel in Coronado. Change came very suddenly to Coronado, a town that did not really want it. (CHA.)

Seven

PRESENT-DAY CORONADO

Coronado has seen much change over the years, but the appeal of this little city remains the same. With a climate envied by the rest of the country, Coronado is alive with activity. People are seen walking the lovely neighborhoods that are full of diverse architecture, beautiful gardens, and historic homes. Bicyclists ride around the perimeter of Coronado, which measures 7 miles. On one side of the "island," San Diego Bay provides endless entertainment as huge navy and cargo ships glide quietly down the harbor. On the other side, Coronado's seemingly endless beach stretches for miles. People watch with fascination as military planes fly overhead and U.S. Navy SEALs run by on the beach.

The City of Coronado maintains thousands of trees, keeping them trimmed and healthy for all to enjoy—a feat that has earned Coronado the designation "Tree City USA" for 25 years, the longest run for any city in San Diego County. The 11-mile stretch of the Silver Strand is home to navy housing, Silver Strand State Park, and the Coronado Cays, and it is also the location of a protected habitat for native birds.

Coronado's local population is about 26,000. Excellent public and private schools provide education for about 4,000 students. Supplied with great city amenities like police and fire protection, public services, the Sharp Coronado Hospital, and multiple grocery stores, many residents do not feel a need to travel over the bridge very often.

The Hotel del Coronado still plays a prominent role in the peninsula's identity. With more than two million visitors a year, tourism is at the heart of Coronado commerce. Home to 17 hotels, including three world-class resorts, more than 70 restaurants, and a world-class beach, it is a repeat destination for visiting families. The combination of navy personnel, tourists, and residents from various backgrounds all share in this peaceful little city, creating an interesting blend of character that completes beautiful and historic Coronado.

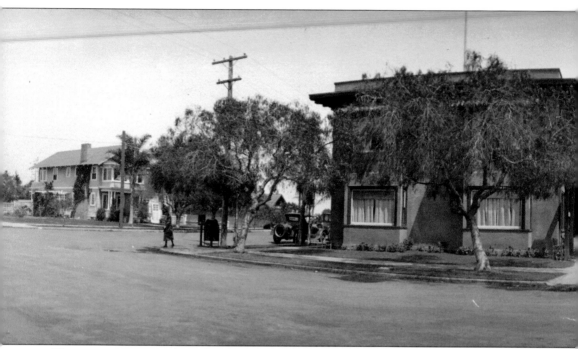

This panoramic picture from the 1920s shows the corner of Tenth Street on A Avenue, a location that looks very similar today. The house at the far left is now painted yellow, and the Vanderbilt and Mission apartments to the center and right, respectively, have been well maintained, with

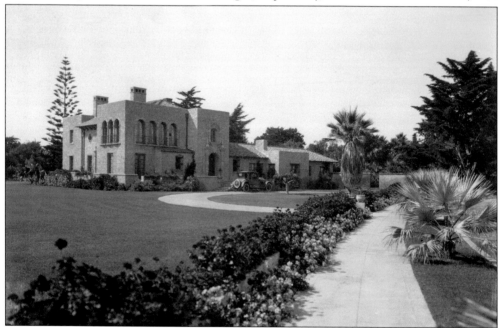

The Rew-Sharp mansion, built in 1919 in the Spanish Colonial Revival style, originally sat on a whole city block next to Ocean Boulevard. The house was eventually divided into two, both of which remain beautiful showcase homes. Sections of the original pebble-coat wall still exist along parts of the block. (SDHC.)

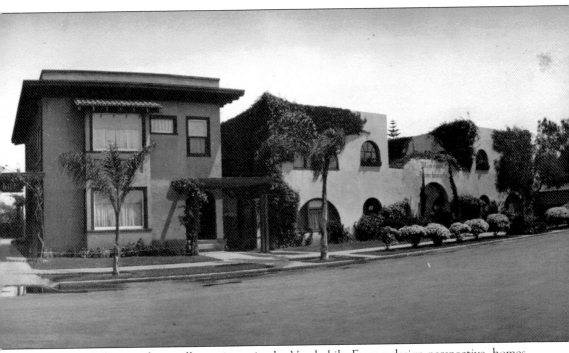

old stained glass windows still prominent in the Vanderbilt. From a design perspective, homes and buildings in Coronado have stood the test of time. (CPL.)

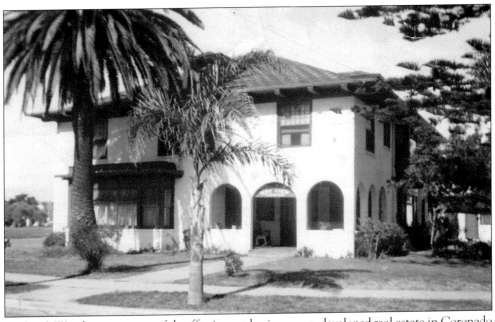

Frederick Winchester, a successful coffee import businessman, developed real estate in Coronado by building craftsman homes, many of which still exist on the 700 block of B Avenue. This home, located at 1060 Adella Avenue, was a boardinghouse bought by Frederick Winchester and his wife, Mary. In recent years, this building was restored as the 1906 Lodge at Coronado Beach, named for the year it was built. (1906 Lodge.)

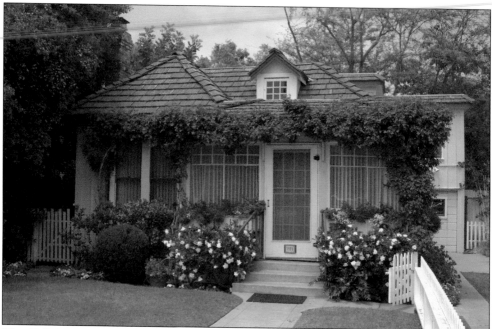

This Folk Victorian home near Star Park is one of the oldest houses in Coronado. The Reid brothers, architects for the Hotel del Coronado and other structures in town, lived here during their tenure on the peninsula. Located on Loma Avenue, this house sits in a neighborhood with other historic homes. (LHC.)

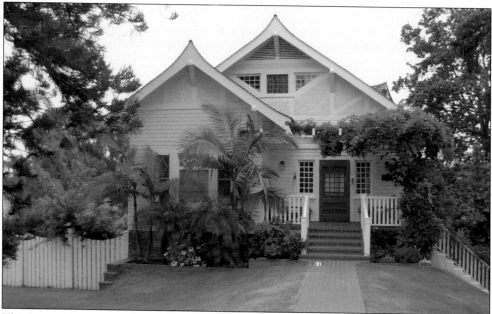

This beautiful house on A Avenue is an example of an old structure that was lovingly restored, with mature trees and plantings around the house. Coronado's diverse architecture is one of the features that make it unique. Though many homes have been lost over the years, many homeowners have worked hard to renovate and maintain the historic houses that are still intact, scattered around Coronado. (LHC.)

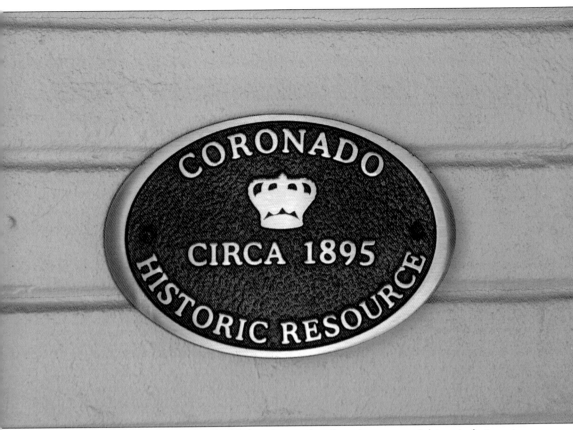

Many older homes around Coronado display plaques detailing the structure's historic designation. A building may be designated as a historic resource based on a combination of the following qualifications: the building is at least 75 years old; it reflects elements specific to Coronado's aesthetic, architectural, cultural, economic, engineering, political, military, or social history; it can be identified with a person or event of significance in local, state, or national history; it is one of a few remaining examples of the architectural style in the city; it is valuable for study of a type, period, or method of construction and has not been substantially altered; or it represents the notable work of an architect, artisan, builder, designer, or landscape professional. Historic designation does not regulate the interior remodel of a residence so homeowners can modify a residence to current living standards, though the designation provides incentive for owners to preserve whenever possible. (LHC.)

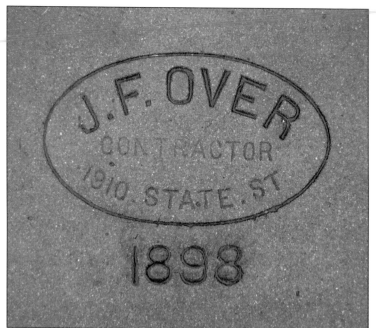

When walking through Coronado's neighborhoods, the sidewalks tell a little story of their own. Concrete stamps are found in sidewalks across Coronado, citing the cement contractor and the year the sidewalk was laid. The City of Coronado makes every effort to save the stamps when sidewalks require replacement by cutting and repouring concrete around the stamp. (LHC.)

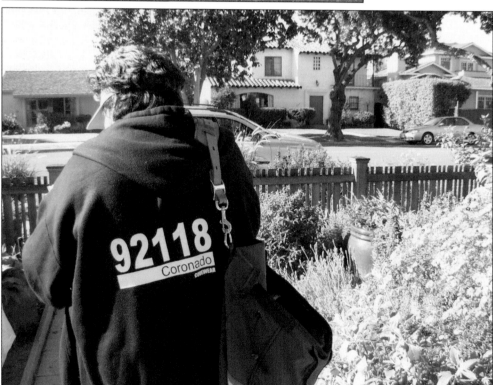

Most longtime residents will say that Coronado has changed dramatically over the years, but they will probably also share many things that have not changed all that much. The quality of life is great, people still keep an eye out for the safety of children, and the postal delivery persons have probably been walking their neighborhood mail routes for years. (LHC.)

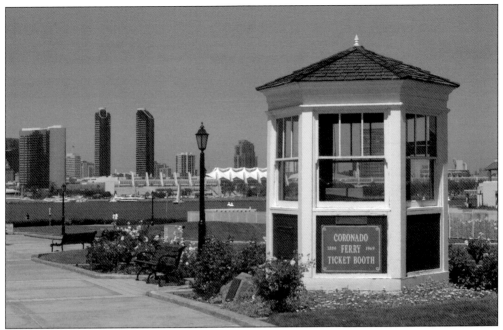

At the foot of Orange Avenue at First Street is Centennial Park, which was dedicated on November 13, 1986, one hundred years after the historic land sale on Coronado. The park now sits where, for 83 years, cars loaded up at the Coronado Ferry Terminal for the trip across San Diego Bay. An original Coronado ferry ticket booth, a reminder of ferry days long gone, is prominently displayed. (LHC.)

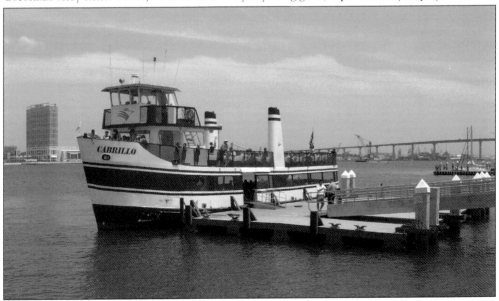

In 1987, when the San Diego-Coronado bridge toll bonds were paid in full, the modern-day passenger ferry was able to launch a new phase of transportation to Coronado. This modern-day passenger ferry arrives and departs from the Coronado Ferry Landing shops, just south of the original ferry piers. Tourists far outnumber residents as riders on the ferry, but commuters from both sides of the bridge make up a regular group of people who ride the ferry every day to get to work. (LHC.)

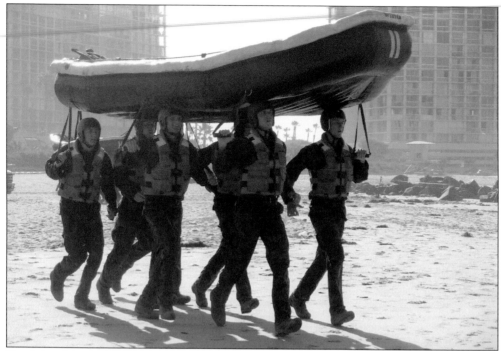

Naval Amphibious Base Coronado (NAB) is home to West Coast Naval Special Warfare Commands. The Naval Special Warfare Center is responsible for basic and advanced SEAL and SWCC training. Basic Underwater Demolition/SEAL (BUD/S) training qualifies individuals as SEALs. Trainees spend months enduring rigorous training. Pictured here are trainees running with an IBS (Inflatable Boat Small) while practicing rock portage in front of the Hotel del Coronado. (LHC.)

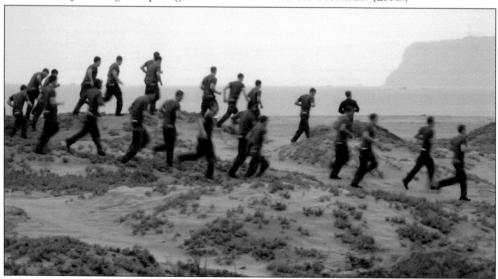

Coronado is sandwiched between the two naval installations of Naval Base Coronado, weaving an interesting mix of community, military, and tourism. Military families from all over the country live in Coronado. "Welcome Home" signs, squadron flyovers, or an aircraft carrier with its deck lined with sailors are all signals of the end of deployment. Coronado is a patriotic town, proud of its servicemen and women. (LHC.)

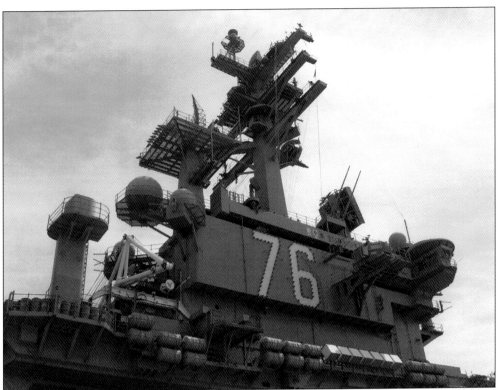

The USS *Ronald Reagan* (CVN-76) is one of three aircraft carriers stationed in Coronado; the other two are the USS *Nimitz* (CVN-68) and the USS *Carl Vinson* (CVN-70). North Island is home to the Commander Naval Air Force U.S. Pacific Fleet and a number of helicopter squadrons, as well as support facilities. In 1997, North Island and the Naval Amphibious Base, as well as other neighboring installations, were combined under the leadership of one commanding officer. Naval Base Coronado's mission is to arm, repair, service, and support the U.S. Pacific Fleet and other operating forces. Employing more than 36,000 military and civilian personnel, the naval base accounts for more than 30 percent of the region's total workforce. (Both, LHC.)

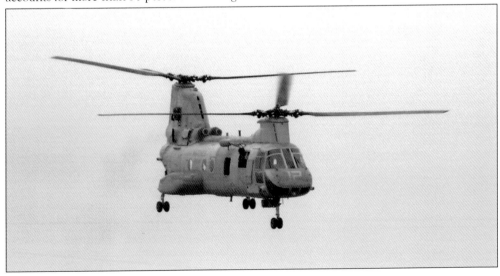

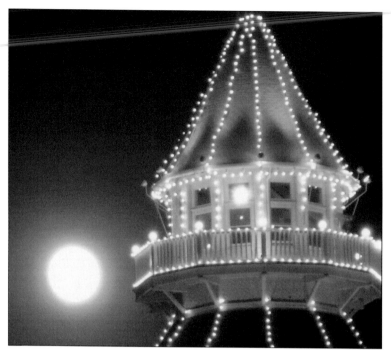

Hotel del Coronado is California-designated Historic Landmark No. 144, dedicated on December 17, 1970. It received National Historic designation on May 5, 1977, and is one of the oldest and largest all-wooden buildings in the United States. During the holiday season, thousands of lights decorate the hotel, making it look like a little jewel from the view at the crest of the Coronado Bridge. (LHC.)

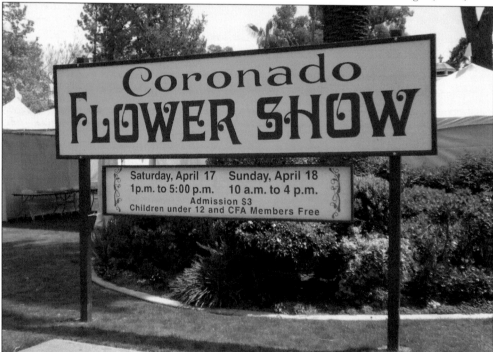

Sponsored by the City of Coronado and the Coronado Floral Association, the Coronado Flower Show is held every year in April. Having the distinction of being the largest tented flower show west of the Mississippi, it is one of Coronado's longest-running traditions since 1922. Hundreds of volunteers work hard to set up a show that includes horticulture, design, and youth sections, as well as educational exhibits. (LHC.)

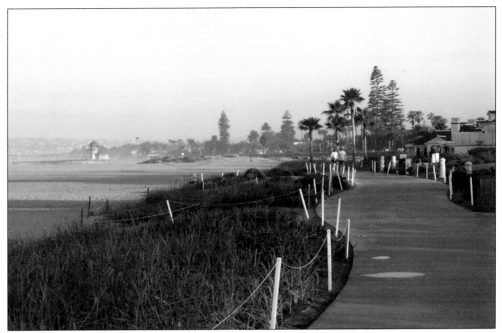

Coronado offers wide streets, nice sidewalks, walking paths, and bike trails. Pedestrians and bicyclists can walk or ride from the ocean to the bay in minutes, down tree-lined streets. The seaside walk at the Hotel del Coronado provides a beautiful stroll along the beach, with access from Ocean Boulevard south to the Coronado Shores. (LHC.)

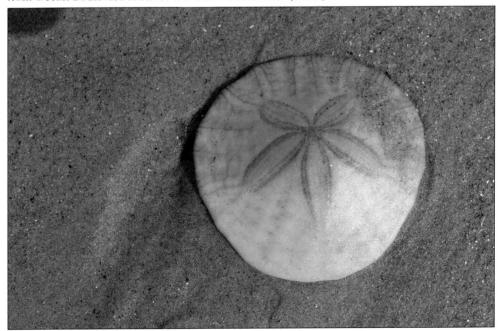

Beachcombing is a favorite pastime in Coronado with miles of beach to walk year-round. Sand dollar beds can be found in shallow waters, making it common to find these fragile treasures. Gold specks seen in the sand are mica that washed down the Tijuana River from the mountains in Mexico and were transported north to Coronado beaches by the Silver Strand littoral current. (LHC.)

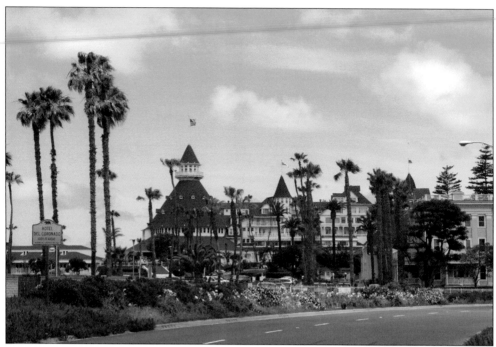

Coronado visitors and residents enjoy the great outdoors all year long. Active people enjoy walking, running, bike riding, swimming, surfing, and golfing, just to name a few popular activities—all of which offer glimpses of Coronado's remarkable scenery. (LHC.)

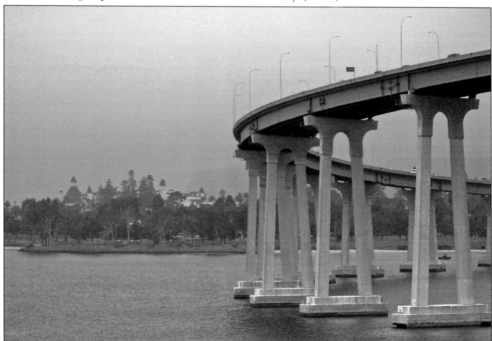

This view of the Coronado Bridge with Hotel del Coronado in the background epitomizes the feeling visitors and residents get as they crest the bridge and look down upon this quaint city. In the springtime, little splashes of purple—jacaranda trees in bloom—polka dot the city. (LHC.)

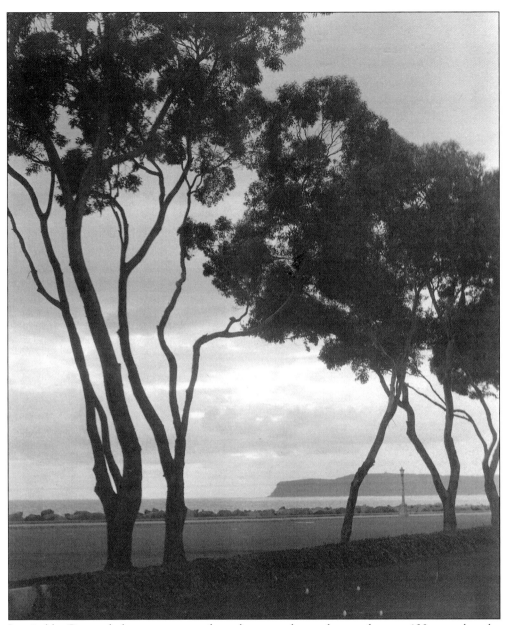

Inevitably, Coronado has seen tremendous change and growth over the past 130 years, but the beauty and special character of this little city is still at large for all who pass through or live here. Tourism and the U.S. Navy are the lifeblood of Coronado, and residents recognize the importance of a vital local economy while still maintaining the desire to keep their city balanced and fair for its citizens. Everyday life in Coronado today is reminiscent of the Crown City's past, where neighbors know each other, strangers take the time to say hello, and the natural splendor of this community can be seen at every turn. The area's culture and quality of life is coveted by all who love Coronado. This view of Point Loma at sunset, taken in the 1920s, is not much different from sitting on the rocks on Ocean Boulevard today, watching another day come to a peaceful end. (CHA.)

Discover Thousands of Local History Books
Featuring Millions of Vintage Images

Arcadia Publishing, the leading local history publisher in the United States, is committed to making history accessible and meaningful through publishing books that celebrate and preserve the heritage of America's people and places.

Find more books like this at
www.arcadiapublishing.com

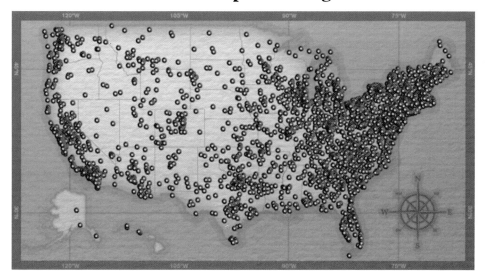

Search for your hometown history, your old stomping grounds, and even your favorite sports team.

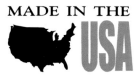